Ghosts of the Trianon

C. A. Moberley and Elinor F. Jourdain

Must Have Books
503 Deerfield Place
Victoria, BC
V9B 6G5
Canada
trava2911@gmail.com

ISBN: 9781774642030

Copyright 2021 – Must Have Books

PREFACE

IT is a great venture to speak openly of a personal experience, and we only do so for the following reasons. First, we prefer that our story, which is known in part to some, should be wholly known as told by ourselves. Secondly, we have collected so much evidence on the subject, that it is possible now to consider it as a whole. Thirdly, conditions are changing at Versailles, and in a short time facts which were unknown, and circumstances which were unusual, may soon become commonplaces, and will lose their force as evidence that some curious psychological conditions must have been present, either in ourselves, or in the place.

It is not our business to explain or to understand—nor do we pretend to understand—what happened to put us into communication with so many true facts, which, nine years ago, no one could have told us of in their entirety. But, in order that others may be able to judge fairly of all the circumstances, we have tried to record exactly what happened as simply and fully as possible.

ELIZABETH MORISON.
FRANCES LAMONT.

PUBLISHERS' NOTE

THE ladies whose Adventure is described in these pages have for various reasons preferred not to disclose their real names, but the signatures appended to the Preface are the only fictitious words in the book. The Publishers guarantee that the Authors have put down what happened to them as faithfully and accurately as was in their power.

CHAPTER I

VISITS TO THE PETIT TRIANON

Miss Morison's Account of the First Visit to the Petit Trianon

AUGUST, 1901

AFTER some days of sight-seeing in Paris, to which we were almost strangers, on an August afternoon, 1901, Miss Lamont and I went to Versailles. We had very hazy ideas as to where it was or what there was to be seen. Both of us thought it might prove to be a dull expedition. We went by train, and walked through the rooms and galleries of the Palace with interest, though we constantly regretted our inability through ignorance to feel properly the charm of the place. My knowledge of French history was limited to the very little I had learnt in the schoolroom, historical novels, and the first volume of Justin M'Carthy's *French Revolution*. Over thirty years before my brother had written a prize poem on *Marie Antoinette*, for whom at the time I had felt much enthusiasm. But the German occupation was chiefly in our minds, and Miss Lamont and I thought and spoke of it several times.

We sat down in the Salle des Glaces, where a very sweet air was blowing in at the open windows over the flower-beds below, and finding that there was time to spare, I suggested our going to the Petit Trianon. My sole knowledge of it was from a magazine article read as a girl, from which I received a general impression that it was a farmhouse where the Queen had amused herself.

Looking in Baedeker's map we saw the sort of direction and that there were two Trianons, and set off. By not asking the way we went an unnecessarily long way round,—by the great flights of steps from the fountains and down the central avenue as far as the head of the long pond. The weather had been very hot all the week, but on this day the sky was a little overcast and the sun shaded. There was a lively wind blowing, the woods were looking their best, and we both felt particularly vigorous. It was a most enjoyable walk.

After reaching the beginning of the long water we struck away to the right down a woodland glade until we came obliquely to the other water close to the building, which we rightly concluded to be the Grand Trianon. We passed it on our left hand, and came up a broad green drive perfectly deserted. If we had followed it we should have come immediately to the Petit Trianon, but not knowing its position, we crossed the drive and went up a lane in front of us. I was surprised that Miss Lamont did not ask the way from a woman who was shaking a white cloth out of the window of a building at the corner of the lane, but followed, supposing that she knew where she was going to. Talking about England and mutual acquaintances there, we went up the lane, and then made a sharp turn to the right past some buildings. We looked in at an open doorway and saw the end of a carved staircase, but as no one was about we did not like to go in. There were three paths in front of us, and as we saw two men a little ahead on the centre one, we followed it, and asked them the way. Afterwards we spoke of them as gardeners, because we remembered a wheelbarrow of some kind close by and the look of a pointed spade, but they were really very dignified officials, dressed in long greyish-green coats with small three-cornered hats. They directed us straight on.

We walked briskly forward, talking as before, but from the moment we left the lane an extraordinary depression had come over me, which, in spite of every effort to shake off, steadily deepened. There seemed to be absolutely no reason for it; I was not at all tired, and was becoming more interested in my surroundings. I was anxious that my companion should not discover the sudden gloom upon my spirits, which became quite overpowering on reaching the point where the path ended, being crossed by another, right and left.

In front of us was a wood, within which, and overshadowed by trees, was a light garden kiosk, circular, and like a small bandstand, by which a man was sitting. There was no green sward, but the ground was covered with rough grass and dead leaves as in a wood. The place was so shut in that we could not see beyond it. Everything suddenly looked unnatural, therefore unpleasant; even the trees behind the building seemed to have become flat and lifeless, *like a wood worked in tapestry.* There were no effects of light and shade, and no wind stirred the trees. It was all intensely still.

The man sitting close to the kiosk (who had on a cloak and a large shady hat) turned his head and looked at us. That was the culmination of my peculiar sensations, and I felt a moment of genuine alarm. The man's face was most repulsive,—its expression odious. His complexion was very dark and rough. I said to Miss Lamont, "Which is our way?" but thought "nothing will induce me to go to the left." It was a great relief at that moment to hear someone running up to us in breathless haste. Connecting the sound with the gardeners, I turned and ascertained that there was no one on the paths, either to the side or behind; but at almost the same moment I suddenly perceived another man quite close to us, behind and rather to the left hand, who had, apparently, just come either over or through the rock (or whatever it was) that shut out the view at the junction of the paths. The suddenness of his appearance was something of a shock.

The second man was distinctly a gentleman; he was tall, with large dark eyes, and had crisp, curling black hair under the same large sombrero hat. He was handsome, and the effect of the hair was to make him look like an old picture. His face was glowing red as through great exertion,—as though he had come a long way. At first I thought he was sunburnt, but a second look satisfied me that the colour was from heat, not sunburning. He had on a dark cloak wrapped across him like a scarf, one end flying out in his prodigious hurry. He looked greatly excited as he called out to us, "Mesdames, Mesdames," or ("Madame" pronounced more as the other), "il ne faut (pronounced *fout*) pas passer par là." He then waved his arm, and said with great animation, "par ici . . . cherchez la maison."[1]

I was so surprised at his eagerness that I looked up at him again, and to this he responded with a little backward movement and

[1] The man said a great deal more which we could not catch.

a most peculiar smile. Though I could not follow all he said, it was clear that he was determined that we should go to the right and not to the left. As this fell in with my own wish, I went instantly towards a little bridge on the right, and turning my head to join Miss Lamont in thanking him, found, to my surprise, that he was not there, but the running began again and from the sound it was close beside us.

Silently we passed over the small rustic bridge which crossed a tiny ravine. So close to us when on the bridge that we could have touched it with our right hands, a thread-like cascade fell from a height down a green pretty bank, where ferns grew between stones. Where the little trickle of water went to I did not see, but it gave me the impression that we were near other water, though I saw none.

Beyond the little bridge our pathway led under trees; it skirted a narrow meadow of long grass, bounded on the further side by trees, and very much overshadowed by trees growing in it. This gave the whole place a sombre look suggestive of dampness, and shut out the view of the house until we were close to it. The house was a square, solidly-built small country house ; — quite different from what I expected. The long windows looking north into the English garden (where we were) were shuttered. There was a terrace round the north and west sides of the house, and on the rough grass which grew quite up to the terrace and with her back to it, a lady was sitting, holding out a paper as though to look at it at arm's length. I supposed her to be sketching, and to have brought her own camp-stool. It seemed as though she must be making a study of trees, for they grew close in front of her, and there seemed to be nothing else to sketch. She saw us, and when we passed close by on her left hand, she turned and looked full at us. It was not a young face, and (though rather pretty) it did not attract me She had on a shady white hat perched on a good deal of fair hair that fluffed round her forehead. Her light summer dress was arranged on her shoulders in handkerchief fashion, and there was a little line of either green or gold near the edge of the handkerchief, which showed me that it was *over*, not tucked into, her bodice, which was cut low. Her dress was long-waisted, with a good deal of fullness in the skirt, which seemed to be short. I thought she was a tourist, but that her dress was old-fashioned and rather unusual (though people were wearing fichu bodices that summer). I looked straight at her; but some indescribable feeling made me turn away annoyed at her being there.

We went up the steps on to the terrace, my impression being that they led up direct from the English garden; but I was beginning to feel as though we were walking in a dream,—the stillness and oppressiveness were so unnatural. Again I saw the lady, this time from behind, and noticed that her fichu was pale green. It was rather a relief to me that Miss Lamont did not propose to ask her whether we could enter the house from that side.

We crossed the terrace to the south-west corner and looked over into the cour d'honneur; and then turned back, and seeing that one of the long windows overlooking the French garden was unshuttered, we were going towards it when we were interrupted. The terrace was prolonged at right angles in front of what seemed to be a second house. The door of it suddenly opened, and a young man stepped out on to the terrace, banging the door behind him. He had the jaunty manner of a footman, but no livery, and called to us, saying that the way into the house was by the cour d'honneur, and offered to show us the way round. He looked inquisitively amused as he walked by us down the French garden till we came to an entrance into the front drive. We came out sufficiently near the first lane we had been in to make me wonder why the garden officials had not directed us back instead of telling us to go forward.

When we were in the front entrance hall we were kept waiting for the arrival of a merry French wedding party. They walked arm in arm in a long procession round the rooms, and we were at the back,—too far off from the guide to hear much of his story. We were very much interested, and felt quite lively again. Coming out of the cour d'honneur we took a little carriage which was standing there, and drove back to the Hotel des Réservoirs in

Versailles, where we had tea[1]; but we were neither of us inclined to talk, and did not mention any of the events of the afternoon. After tea we walked back to the station, looking on the way for the Tennis Court.

On the way back to Paris the setting sun at last burst out from under the clouds, bathing the distant Versailles woods in glowing light, —Valerien standing out in front a mass of deep purple. Again and again the thought returned,—Was Marie Antoinette really much at Trianon, and did she see it for the last time long before the fatal drive to Paris accompanied by the mob?

For a whole week we never alluded to that afternoon, nor did I think about it until I began writing a descriptive letter of our expeditions of the week before. As the scenes came back one by one, the same sensation of dreamy unnatural oppression came over me so strongly that I stopped writing, and said to Miss Lamont, "Do you think that the Petit Trianon is haunted?" Her answer was prompt,

[1] I remember that on account of the wind I put on my coat.

"Yes, I do." I asked her where she felt it, and she said, " In the garden where we met the two men, but not only there." She then described her feeling of depression and anxiety which began at the same point as it did with me, and how she tried not to let me know it. Talking it over we fully realised, for the first time, the theatrical appearance of the man who spoke to us, the inappropriateness of the wrapped cloak on a warm summer afternoon, the unaccountableness of his coming and going, the excited running which seemed to begin and end close to us, and yet always out of sight, and the extreme earnestness with which he desired us to go one way and not another. I said that the thought had crossed my mind that the two men were going to fight a duel, and that they were waiting until we were gone. Miss Lamont owned to having disliked the thought of passing the man of the kiosk.

We did not speak again of the incident during my stay in Paris, though we visited the Conciergerie prisons, and the tombs of Louis XVI. and Marie Antoinette at Saint Denis, where all was clear and fresh and natural.

Three months later Miss Lamont came to stay with me, and on Sunday, November 10th, 1901, we returned to the subject, and I said, " If we had known that a lady was sitting so near us sketching it would have made all the difference, for we should have asked the way." She replied that she had seen no lady. I reminded her of the person sitting under the terrace; but Miss Lamont declared that there was no one there. I exclaimed that it was impossible that she should not have seen the individual; for we were walking side by side and went straight up to her, passed her and looked down upon her from the terrace. It was inconceivable to us both that she should not have seen the lady, but the fact was clear that Miss Lamont had not done so, though we had both been rather on the lookout for someone who would reassure us as to whether we were trespassing or not.

Finding that we had a new element of mystery, and doubting how far we had seen any of the same things, we resolved to write down independent accounts of our expedition to Trianon, read up its history, and make every enquiry about the place. Miss Lamont returned to her school the same evening, and two days later I received from her a very interesting letter, giving the result of her first enquiries.

E. M.

Miss Lamont's Account of her First Visit
to the Petit Trianon in 1901

AUGUST, 1901

IN the summer of 1900 I stayed in Paris for
the first time, and in the course of that summer
took a flat and furnished it, intending to place a
French lady there in charge of my elder school-
girls. Paris was quite new to me, and beyond
seeing the picture galleries and one or two
churches I made no expeditions except to shops,
for the Exhibition of 1900 was going on, and
all my free time was spent in seeing it with my
French friends. The next summer, however,
1901, when, after several months at my school
in England, I came back to Paris, it was to
take the first opportunity possible of having a
visitor to stay there : and I asked Miss Morison
to come with me.

Miss Morison suggested our seeing the his-
toric part of Paris in something like chrono-
logical order, and I looked forward to seeing it

practically for the first time with her. We decided to go to Versailles one day, though rather reluctantly, as we felt it was diverging from our plan to go there too soon. I did not know what to expect, as my ignorance of the place and its significance was extreme. So we looked up general directions in Baedeker, and trusted to finding our way at the time.

After spending some time in the Palace, we went down by the terrace and struck to the right to find the Petit Trianon. We walked for some distance down a wooded alley, and then came upon the buildings of the Grand Trianon, before which we did not delay. We went on in the direction of the Petit Trianon, but just before reaching what we knew afterwards to be the main entrance I saw a gate leading to a path cut deep below the level of the ground above, and as the way was open and had the look of an entrance that was used, I said: "Shall we try this path? it must lead to the house," and we followed it. To our right we saw some farm-buildings looking empty and deserted; implements (among others a plough) were lying about; we looked in, but saw no one. The impression was saddening, but it was not until we reached the crest of the rising ground where there was a garden that I began to feel as if we had lost our way, and as if something were wrong. There were two men there in official dress (greenish in colour), with something in their hands; it might have been a staff. A wheelbarrow and some other gardening tools were near them. They told us, in answer to my enquiry, to go straight on. I remember repeating my question, because they answered in a seemingly casual and mechanical way, but only got the same answer in the same manner. As we were standing there I saw to the right of us a detached solidly-built cottage, with stone steps at the door. A woman and a girl were standing at the doorway, and I particularly noticed their unusual dress; both wore white kerchiefs tucked into the bodice, and the girl's dress, though she looked 13 or 14 only, was down to her ankles. The woman was passing a jug to the girl, who wore a close white cap.[1]

[1] The woman was standing on the steps, bending slightly forward, holding a jug in her hand. The girl was looking up at her from below with her hands raised, but nothing in them. She might have been just going to take the jug or have just given it up. Her light-brown hair escaped from under her

B

Following the directions of the two men we walked on: but the path pointed out to us seemed to lead away from where we imagined the Petit Trianon to be; and there was a feeling of depression and loneliness about the place. I began to feel as if I were walking in my sleep; the heavy dreaminess was oppressive. At last we came upon a path crossing ours, and saw in front of us a building consisting of some columns roofed in, and set back in the trees. Seated on the steps was a man with a heavy black cloak round his shoulders, and wearing a slouch hat. At that moment the eerie feeling which had begun in the garden culminated in a definite impression of something uncanny and fear-inspiring. The man slowly turned his face, which was marked by smallpox: his complexion was very dark. The expression was very evil and yet unseeing, and though I did not feel that he was looking particularly at us, I felt a repugnance to going past him. But I did not wish to show the feeling, which I thought was meaningless, and we talked about the

cap. I remember that both seemed to pause for an instant, as in a *tableau vivant*; but we passed on, and I did not see the end.

best way to turn, and decided to go to the right.

Suddenly we heard a man running behind us: he shouted, "Mesdames, mesdames," and when I turned he said in an accent that seemed to me unusual that our way lay in another direction. " Il ne faut (pronounced *fout*) pas passer par là." He then made a gesture, adding "par ici . . . cherchez la maison." Though we were surprised to be addressed, we were glad of the direction, and I thanked him. The man ran off with a curious smile on his face : the running ceased as abruptly as it had begun, not far from where we stood. I remember that the man was young-looking, with a florid complexion and rather long dark hair. I do not remember the dress, except that the material was dark and heavy, and that the man wore buckled shoes.

We walked on, crossing a small bridge that went across a green bank, high on our right hand and shelving down below as to a very small overshadowed pool of water glimmering some way off. A tiny stream descended from above us, so small as to seem to lose itself before reaching the little pool. We then followed a narrow path till almost immediately we came upon the English garden front of the Petit Trianon. The place was deserted; but as we approached the terrace I remember drawing my skirt away with a feeling as though someone were near and I had to make room, and then wondering why I did it. While we were on the terrace a boy came out of the door of a second building which opened on it, and I still have the sound in my ears of his slamming it behind him. He directed us to go round to the other entrance, and seeing us hesitate, with the peculiar smile of suppressed mockery, offered to show us the way. We passed through the French garden, part of which was walled in by trees. The feeling of dreariness was very strong there, and continued till we actually reached the front entrance to the Petit Trianon and looked round the rooms in the wake of a French wedding party. Afterwards we drove back to the Rue des Réservoirs.

The impression returned to me at intervals during the week that followed, but I did not speak of it until Miss Morison asked me if I thought the Petit Trianon was haunted, and I said Yes. Then, too, the inconsistency of the dress and behaviour of the man with an August afternoon at Versailles struck me. We had only this one conversation about the two men. Nothing else passed between us in Paris.

It was not till three months later, when I was staying with her, that Miss Morison casually mentioned the lady, and almost refused to believe that I had not seen her. How that happened was quite inexplicable to me, for I believed myself to be looking about on all sides, and it was not so much that I did not remember her as that I could have said no one was there. But as she said it I remembered my impression at the moment of there being more people than I could see, though I did not tell her this.

The same evening, November 10th, 1901, I returned to my school near London. Curiously enough, the next morning I had to give one of a set of lessons on the French Revolution for the Higher Certificate, and it struck me for the first time with great interest that the 10th of August had a special significance in French history, and that we had been at Trianon on the anniversary of the day.

That evening when I was preparing to write down my experiences, a French friend whose home was in Paris came into my room, and I asked her, just on the chance, if she knew any story about the haunting of the Petit Trianon. (I had not mentioned our story to her before, nor indeed to anyone.) She said directly that she remembered hearing from friends at Versailles that on a certain day in August Marie Antoinette is regularly seen sitting outside the garden front at the Petit Trianon, with a light flapping hat and a pink dress. More than this, that the place, especially the farm, the garden, and the path by the water, are peopled with those who used to be with her there ; in fact that all the occupations and amusements reproduce themselves there for a day and a night. I then told her our story, and when I quoted the words that the man spoke to us, and imitated as well as I could his accent, she immediately said that it was the Austrian pronunciation of French. I had privately thought that he spoke old[1] French. Immediately afterwards I wrote and told this to Miss Morison.

F. L.

[1] By old I mean old or unusual forms, perhaps surviving in provincial French.

On receiving Miss Lamont's letter I turned to my diary to see on what Saturday in August it was that we had visited Versailles, and looked up the history to find out to what event she alluded. On August 10th, 1792, the Tuileries was sacked. The royal family escaped in the early morning to the Hall of the Assembly, where they were penned up for many hours hearing themselves deposed, and within sound of the massacre of their servants and of the Swiss guards at the Tuileries. From the Hall the King and Queen were taken to the Temple.

We wondered whether we had inadvertently entered within an act of the Queen's memory when alive, and whether this explained our curious sensation of being completely shut in and oppressed. What more likely, we thought, than that during those hours in the Hall of the Assembly, or in the Conciergerie, she had gone back in such vivid memory to other Augusts spent at Trianon that some impress of it was imparted to the place? Some pictures which were shown to me proved that the out-door dress of the gentlemen at Court had been a large hat and cloak, and that the ladies wore long-waisted bodices, with full gathered short skirts, fichus, and hats.

I told the story to my brother, and we heartily agreed that, as a rule, such stories made no impression at all upon us, because we always believed that, if only the persons involved would take the trouble to investigate them thoroughly and honestly for themselves, they could be quite naturally explained. We agreed that such a story as ours had very little value without more proof of reality than it had, but that as there were one or two interesting points in it, it would be best to sift the matter quietly, lest others should make more of them than they deserved. He suggested lightly and in fun that perhaps we had seen the Queen as she thought of herself, and that it would be interesting to know whether the dress described was the one she had on at the time of her rêverie, or whether it was one she recollected having worn at an earlier date. My brother also enquired whether we were quite sure that the last man we had seen (who came out of the side building), as well as the wedding party, were all real persons. I assured him with great amusement that we had not the smallest doubt as to the reality of them all.

As Miss Lamont was going to Paris for the Christmas holidays, I wrote and asked her to take any opportunity she might have to see the place again, and to make a plan of the paths and the buildings ; for the guide books spoke of the Temple de l'Amour and the Belvédère, and I thought one of them might prove to be our kiosk.

E. M.

Miss Lamont's Account of her Second Visit
to the Petit Trianon

JANUARY, 1902

ON January 2nd, 1902, I went for the second
time to Versailles.   It was a cold and wet day,
but I was anxious not to be deterred by that, as
it was likely to be my only possible day that
winter.   This time I drove straight to the
Petit Trianon, passing the Grand Trianon.
Here I could see the path up which we had
walked in August.   I went, however, to the
regular entrance, thinking I would go at once to
the Temple de l'Amour, even if I had time to go
no further.   To the right of the cour d'honneur
was a door in the wall ; it led to the Hameau
de la Reine and to the gardens.   I took this
path and came to the Temple de l'Amour,
which was *not* the building we had passed in
the summer.   There was, so far, none of the
eerie feeling we had experienced in August.
But, on crossing a bridge to go to the Hameau,

the old feeling returned in full force; it was as if I had crossed a line and was suddenly in a circle of influence. To the left I saw a tract of park-like ground, the trees bare and very scanty. I noticed a cart being filled with sticks by two labourers, and thought I could go to them for directions if I lost my way. The men wore tunics and capes with pointed hoods of bright colours, a sort of terra-cotta red and deep blue.[1] I turned aside for an instant—not more—to look at the Hameau, and when I looked back men and cart were completely out of sight, and this surprised me, as I could see a long way in every direction. And though I had seen the men in the act of loading the cart with sticks, I could not see any trace of them on the ground either at the time or afterwards. I did not, however, dwell upon any part of the incident, but went on to the Hameau. The houses were all built near a sheet of water, and the old oppressive feeling of the last year was noticeable, especially under the balcony of the Maison de la Reine, and near a window in what I afterwards found to be the Laiterie.

[1] One man wore red, the other blue; the colours were not mixed.

I really felt a great reluctance to go near the window or look in, and when I did so I found it shuttered inside.

Coming away from the Hameau I at last reached a building, which I knew from my plan to be the smaller Orangerie; then, meaning to go to the Belvédère, I turned back by mistake into the park and found myself in a wood, so thick that though I had turned towards the Hameau I could not see it. Before I entered I looked across an open space towards a belt of trees to the left of the Hameau some way off, and noticed a man, cloaked like those we had seen before, slip swiftly through the line of trees. The smoothness of his movement attracted my attention.

I was puzzling my way among the maze of paths in the wood when I heard a rustling behind me which made me wonder why people in silk dresses came out on such a wet day; and I said to myself, "just like French people." I turned sharply round to see who they were, but saw no one, and then, all in a moment, I had the same feeling as by the terrace in the summer, only in a much greater degree; it was as though I were closed in by a group of people who already filled the path, coming from behind and passing me. At one moment there seemed really no room for me. I heard some women's voices talking French, and caught the words "Monsieur et Madame" said close to my ear. The crowd got scarce and drifted away, and then faint music as of a band, not far off, was audible. It was playing very light music with a good deal of repetition in it. Both voices and music were diminished in tone, as in a phonograph, unnaturally. The pitch of the band was lower than usual. The sounds were intermittent, and once more I felt the swish of a dress close by me.

I looked at the map which I had with me, but whenever I settled which path to take I felt impelled to go by another. After turning backwards and forwards many times I at last found myself back at the Orangerie, and was overtaken by a gardener.[1] I asked him where I should find the Queen's grotto, that had been

---

[1] I thought this gardener did not look like a Frenchman ; he had more the air of an Englishman. He had hair on his face, a grizzled beard, was large and loosely made. His height was very uncommon, and he seemed to be of immense strength. His arms were long and very muscular. I noticed that even through the sleeves of his jersey.

mentioned in De Nolhac's book which I had
procured while in Paris. He told me to follow
the path I was on, and, in answer to a question,
said that I must pass the Belvédère, adding
that it was quite impossible to find one's way
about the park unless one had been brought up
in the place, and so used to it that "personne
ne pourrait vous tromper." The expression
specially impressed me because of the experience I had just had in the wood. He pointed
out the way and left me. The path led past
the Belvédère, which I took for granted was
the building we had seen in August, for coming
upon it from behind, all the water was hidden
from me. I made my way from there to the
French garden without noticing the paths I
took.

On my return to Versailles I made careful
enquiries as to whether the band had been
playing there that day, but was told that though
it was the usual day of the week, it had not
played because it had played the day before,
being New Year's Day.

I told my French friends of my walk, and they
said that there was a tradition of Marie Antoinette having been seen making butter within the

Laiterie, and for that reason it was shuttered. A second tradition they mentioned interested me very much. It was that on October 5th, 1789—which was the last day on which Marie Antoinette went to Trianon—she was sitting there in her grotto, and saw a page running towards her, bringing the letter from the minister at the palace to say that the mob from Paris would be at the gates in an hour's time. The story went on that she impulsively proposed walking straight back to the palace by the short cut through the trees. He would not allow it : but begged her to go to the "maison" to wait whilst he fetched the carriage by which she was generally conveyed back through the park, and that he ran off to order it.

F. L.

January, 1902.

1902-4.

DURING the next two years very little occurred to throw light on the story. The person living in Versailles to whom we had been directed as having related the tradition of the Queen's being at Trianon on October 5th, 1789, was unable to remember anything at all about it. The photographs of the Belvédère made it clear that it was not identical with the kiosk. On the many occasions on which Miss Lamont went to the Trianon she could never again find the places,—not even the wood in which she had been. She assured me that the place was entirely different; the distances were much less than we had imagined; and the ground was so bare that the house and the Hameau were in full view of one another; and that there was nothing unnatural about the trees.

Miss Lamont brought back from Paris *La Reine Marie Antoinette*, by M. de Nolhac, and *Le Petit Trianon*, by Desjardins. We noted that M. de Nolhac related the traditional story of the Queen's visit, and that the Comte de Vaudreuil, who betrayed the Queen by inviting her to the fatal acting of the "Barbier de Séville" in her own theatre at Trianon, was a Creole and marked by small-pox (pages 61, 212). Turning over the pages of Desjardins I found Wertmüller's portrait of the Queen, and exclaimed that it was the first of all the pictures I had seen which at all brought back the face of the lady. Some weeks later I found this passage: "Ce tableau fut assez mal accueilli des critiques contemporains qui le trouvèrent froid, sans majesté, sans grace. Pour la posterité, au contraire, il a le plus grand mérite; celui de la ressemblance. Au dire de Madame Campan, il n'existe de bon portrait de la reine que cette toile de Wertmüller et celle que Madame Lebrun peignit en 1787" (page 282).

In January, 1904, Miss Lamont went to the Comédie Française to see the "Barbier de Séville," and noticed that the Alguazils standing round were dressed exactly like our garden officials, but had red stockings added. This was interesting, as the Comédie Française

c

is the descendant of the Royal Private Theatre, and the old royal liveries worn by the subordinate actors (who were, in earlier times, the royal servants) are carefully reproduced at it. Also, she reported, that Almaviva was dressed in a dark cloak and a large Spanish hat, which was said to be the outdoor dress of French gentlemen of the period.

E. M.

On Monday, July 4th, 1904, Miss Lamont and I went to the Trianon, this being my second visit. We were accompanied by Mademoiselle ———, who had not heard our story. On the Saturday of the same week (July 9th) we went again unaccompanied.

Both days were brilliant and hot. On both occasions the dust, glare, trams, and comers and goers, were entirely different from the quietness and solitude of our visit in 1901. We went up the lane as at the first time and turned to the right on reaching the building, which we had now learnt to call the *logement des corps de gardes*. From this point everything was changed. The old wall facing us had gates, but they were closed, and the one through which we had seen the drive passing through a grove of trees seemed to have been closed for a very long time. We came directly to the gardener's house, which was quite different in appearance from the cottage described by Miss Lamont in 1901, in front of which she saw the woman and the girl. Beyond the gardener's house was a parterre with flower-beds, and a smooth lawn of many years' careful tendance. It did not seem to be the place where we had met the garden officials.

We spent a long time looking for the old paths. Not only was there no trace of them, but the distances were contracted, and all was on a smaller scale than I recollected. The kiosk was gone ; so was the ravine and the little cascade which had fallen from a height above our heads, and the little bridge over the ravine was, of course, gone too. The large bridge with the *rocher* over it, crossing one side of the lake at the foot of the Belvédère, had no resemblance to it. The trees were quite natural, and seemed to have been a good deal cleared out, making that part of the garden much less wooded and picturesque.

The English garden in front of the house was not shaded by many trees ; and we could see the house and the hameau from almost every point. Instead of a much shaded rough meadow continuing up to the wall of the terrace, there is now a broad gravel sweep beneath it, |and the trees on the grass are gone. Exactly where the lady was sitting we found a large spreading bush of, apparently, many years' growth. We did not recognise the present staircase, which leads up to the north-west end of the terrace, nor the extension of wall round which one has now to go in order to reach the staircase. We thought that we went up to the terrace from some point nearer to the house from the English garden. The present exit from the French garden to the avenue was not so near the house as we expected, nor was it so broad as we remembered it.

To add to the impossibility of recalling our first visit, in every corner we came across groups of noisy merry people walking or sitting in the shade. Garden seats placed everywhere, and stalls for fruit and lemonade took away from any idea of desolation. The common-place, unhistorical atmosphere was totally inconsistent with the air of silent mystery by which we had been so much oppressed. Though for several years Miss Lamont had assured me of the change, I had not expected such complete disillusionment.

One thing struck me greatly—people went wherever they liked, and no one would think of interfering to show the way, or to prevent anyone from going in any direction. We searched the place at our pleasure.

We went to the Hameau, following the path taken by Miss Lamont on January 2, 1902. We tried to find the thick wood in which she had lost her way, but there was nothing like it, and such paths as there are now are perfectly visible from one another, even in summer. We asked a gardener sweeping one of the paths whether that part of the grounds had ever been a thick wood. He said he believed that it had been, but could give us no date beyond the fact that it was before his time—more than twenty years ago.

On our return to Versailles, we went into a bookseller's shop and asked if he had any maps or views of the Petit Trianon as it had been in old days. He showed us a picture (which he would not part with) of the Jeu de Bague. We saw at once that the central building had some likeness to the kiosk, but the surrounding part was not like, and its position was unsuitable for our purpose. We enquired about the green uniforms of the garden officials, and he emphatically denied their existence. He said that "green was one of the colours of the royal liveries," and when we answered that three years before persons in long green coats had directed us in the grounds, he spoke of it as "impossible, unless (he added) they were masqueraders." One of the *gardiens* of the Palace also told us that "green was a royal livery and that now only the President had the right to use it on certain occasions."

We asked how long the gardens had been thrown open to the public and people allowed to wander everywhere, and were told that "it had been so for *years*," and this evidently implied a great many years.

The result of this visit was to make us take a graver view of the two first visits, and we resolved to look into the matter as carefully as we could, and to be entirely silent about the change of scenery until we had explained it somewhat to ourselves. After some years, and in spite of various false leads, we have been able to put together some very interesting facts. The details of the search are recorded in a book which, to us, goes by the name of the Green Book. It contains the original papers written in 1901, the history of the gradual accumulation of information, correspondence with one another and also with others on the subject, the accounts written by one or two friends who have helped us at different times, also pictures, maps, and lists of books consulted, and the account of curious incidents which took place during the search.

E. M.

F. L.

CHAPTER II

SUMMARY OF RESULTS OF RESEARCH

The Plough

THE first incident in our expedition to Trianon in 1901 was that, after passing the *logement des corps de gardes,* a small hand plough was seen by Miss Lamont lying on the ground not far from some wide open gates in an old wall opposite to us, through which we could see the stems of a grove of trees, and a drive leading through it.

In 1905 Miss Lamont was told by a gardener that no plough was kept at Trianon; there was no need of one, as the government only required the lawns, walks, water, trees, and flowers, to be kept up.

In 1908 another gardener told us both that ploughs have entirely altered in character since the Revolution, and it was not likely that the old type would be seen anywhere in France now.

It would seem that no plough was used ordinarily at Trianon even in old days, for amongst a list of tools bought for the gardeners from 1780-1789, there is no mention of a plough.[1]

We learned, in 1905, from Desjardins' book, that throughout the reign of Louis XVI. an old plough used in his predecessor's reign had been preserved at the Petit Trianon and sold with the king's other properties during the Revolution.[2]

A picture of this identical plough, procured in 1907, showed that it had handles like the one seen in 1901, but the cutting part was hidden in the ground and could not be compared.[3]

In the old map of 1783 there is ploughed land where later the Hameau was built and the sheet of water placed : but there is none in the later maps, nor any now to be seen in the grounds.

[1] *Archives Nationales* O¹, 1878.

[2] Desjardins, p. 15 ; Rocheterie's *Histoire de Marie Antoinette*, pp. 289, 290, vol. i.

[3] In the Bibliothèque Nationale.

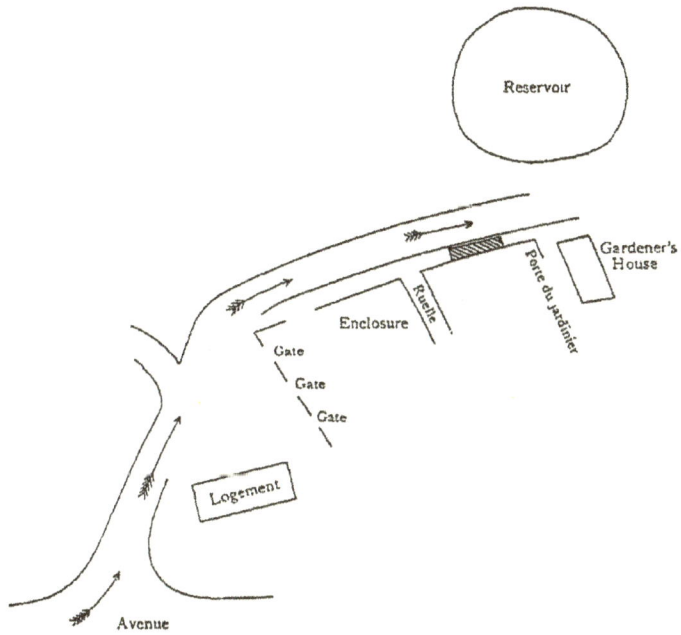

Reservoir

Gardener's
House

Porte du jardinier

Ruelle

Enclosure

Gate

Gate

Gate

Logement

Avenue

The Guards

The second event was our meeting with two dignified, thoughtful-looking officials, dressed in long green coats and three-cornered hats, holding something in their hands which Miss Lamont wrote of in 1901 as possibly being staves. In response to our enquiry for the Petit Trianon they coldly directed us forward.

There are no officials so dressed at Trianon now. At present they wear black, with tricolour rosettes in their hats; in summer they have white trousers.

In 1904 we were told by fully-informed persons at Versailles that it was "impossible" that we should have seen such uniforms, "unless they were worn by masqueraders," for green was a royal livery, and no one wore it now at Trianon.

Supposing them to have been masqueraders, the dress may have been that of *gardes de la porte*. The ceremonial overdress of the *gardes de la porte*, as was that of part of the *gardes du corps* (*gardes de la Manche*), was green, with gold and silver embroidery and red stockings:

they carried halberds.[1]   But the officers had *galon* instead of embroidery, and no red stockings : they carried an ebony cane with an ivory ball.[2]

The livery of the Comte d'Artois, who was *colonel-général* of the *gardes Suisses* was green ; and those of the *gardes du corps* and *Suisses* who were in his service had green uniforms.[3]

There is evidence of a much quieter dress without even *galon*, called the "petite livrée," which was probably green, as it was worn by the *Suisses, piqueurs, gardes de la porte*, and the *garçons jardiniers*.[4]   The traditional dress of those royal servants who filled the minor parts in the Royal Theatre at Versailles is still to be seen at the acting of the *Barbier de Séville* in the Comédie Française, which is the descendant of the Royal Theatre.   This dress (except for the added red stockings) is the same as the one we saw in 1901.

In 1908 we learned that the *porte du jardinier* at the Petit Trianon was always guarded

---

[1] Picture of a Garde de la Porte du Roi Louis XV., dite de la Manche, d'après une gravure de Chevilet. R. Jacquemin.

[2] *Souvenirs d'un Page, le comte D'Hezecques*, pp. 130-134. (He says that their underdress was blue.)

[3] *Ibid.*, p. 137.   [4] *Arch. Nat.* O¹, 1883.

'dans le temps,' and that on October 5th, 1789, the guards were two of the three Bersy brothers who, with Bréval, were generally on duty whenever the Queen was in residence at Trianon. From their writing and spelling they were evidently well educated.[1] In 1910 we found that they had the title of *garçons jardiniers de la Chambre*, and they are said to have been stationed in "*la pepinière proche la maison.*" The most ancient pepinière was close to the gardener's house.

Cottage, Woman, and Girl

Whilst speaking to the two men, Miss Lamont observed on her right hand a solidly-built cottage with stone steps, on which a woman in old-fashioned dress was standing, handing something to a girl of about 13 or 14, who wore a white cap and skirts nearly reaching to her ankles.

In 1904, Miss Lamont saw a picture resembling this cottage in its general appearance in the Album de Trianon at the Bibliothèque nationale. In 1908, she and a friend dis-

[1] *Arch. Nat.* O[1], 1878 and 1880.

covered such a cottage (more than one) within
the gates which were not far from the place
where she had seen the plough. These cottages
were not in the right position for our experience in 1901, but the type was the same.

In 1907 we discovered from the map of 1783
that there was a building, not now in existence,
placed against the wall (outside) of the gardener's yard between the *ruelle* and the *porte
du jardinier*; if our original route lay through
this yard to the English garden, this building
would be exactly in the right place for Miss
Lamont's cottage.

In September, 1910, we saw from marks on
this wall that a building might have stood
here; for the cornice of the wall is broken
into, and there seems to be a perpendicular
line from it to the ground visible through
the plaster. A photograph shows this.

If the girl seen should be the "Marion" of
Madame Julie Lavergne's story (first read in
1906), she would have been 14 years old in
1789, and her mother was then alive. Her
father's house would have been near the reservoir and not within the locked gates of any
enclosure, for she let herself out at night by

an open window.[1] All this would suit the
position of the building in the map.

The Kiosk

On our entrance into the English garden in
1901, we found our path crossed by another,
beyond which, in front of us but rather to the
left hand, stood a small circular building having
pillars and a low surrounding wall. It was on
rough uneven ground, and was overshadowed
by trees.

Repeated searches during seven years by
ourselves and others have failed to discover
this building.

In September, 1908, Miss Lamont found in
the archives a paper (without signature or date)
giving the estimate for a "ruine" having seven
Ionic columns, walls, and a dome roof. (A
"ruine" seems only to mean a copy of an older
building.) If the walls of this building were
low it would correspond in appearance with
our recollection of the kiosk. This "ruine"
is said to have formed a "naissance de la
rivière," suggesting its position above the small

[1] *Légendes de Trianon*, Madame Julie Lavergne, pp. 89, 96.

lake which fed the principal river.[1]   A piece of old water pipe is still to be seen on the north-western side of the small lake.

If this "ruine" and two others of those alluded to in the archives were one and the same, there is additional reason for placing the columned building in this part of the garden. I. In 1788 it is stated that rocks were placed at intervals on a path leading from "la ruine" to the "2ième source du ravin" beyond the wooden bridge.[2]   Desjardins considers one of the "sources" to have been close to the theatre which was at our right hand; this might have been the second spring.[3]   II. Mique states that in 1780 he placed a small architectural "ruine" above the grotto. A note in the archives, dated 1777, speaks of the "porte d'entrée au bout du grotte."[4]   If, as we believe, we had just passed out of the gardener's yard by this "porte d'entrée" we should have been close to the earliest placed grotto.

In 1909 two old maps were procured from Paris; in one, dated 1840 (?), there is something which may indicate a small round building

[1] *Arch. Nat.* O[1], 1878.   [2] *Ibid.* O[1], 1882.
[3] Desjardins, p. 90.   [4] *Arch. Nat.* O[1], 1875.

D

placed on the *rocher* behind the Belvédère. The other map was reproduced from an old one of 1705, but added to until a railway appears in it. In this map below the name "pavillon de musique" (the Belvédère) is the name "Le Kiosque." It does not seem likely that a second name for the Belvédère should be given, and it may therefore refer to something else which does not appear in this map. Therefore the mere chance name which from the first moment we gave to our building was justified by there having been something called by that name exactly in that part of the garden.

In 1910 we looked out this name in the best etymological French dictionary and found that it was admitted to the French Academy in 1762, as "pavillon ouvert de tous côtés" : and defined by Thévenot (contemporary) as "kioch ou divan qui est maintenu de huit grosses colonnes."

The Man by the Kiosk

On our first visit a dark-complexioned man, marked by smallpox, was sitting close to the kiosk; he wore a large dark cloak and a slouch hat.

Though we were assured in 1908 by a very good authority, that no gentleman now living at Versailles would wear a large cloak either in winter or summer, there might be nothing surprising in what we saw if the kiosk could be found. But considering that it is gone, it is historically interesting that we discovered in 1904 that there is one man in the story of Trianon who exactly suits the description.

Most of the intimate accounts of the period say that the Comte de Vaudreuil was a Creole and marked by smallpox.[1] He was at one time one of the Queen's innermost circle of friends, but acted an enemy's part in persuading her to gain the King's permission for the acting of the politically dangerous play of *Le Mariage de Figaro*. The King had long refused to allow it, saying that it would cause the Bastille to be taken. The earlier version of the same play, *Le Barbier de Séville*,[2] was last acted at

---

[1] *La Reine Marie Antoinette*, De Nolhac, pp. 61, 212.

[2] *Le Barbier de Séville*, by Beaumarchais, was first played in 1775 ; it was re-written and made politically scandalous as *Le Mariage de Figaro* in 1781. This version was played in Vaudreuil's private theatre at Gennevilliers and at the Odéon, 1783, and for the first time in Paris, by permission, April 27th, 1784.

Trianon (August 19th, 1785), just at the beginning of the diamond necklace episode, when Vaudreuil took the part of Almaviva and was dressed for it in a large dark cloak and Spanish hat.

In 1908 we found out from Madame Éloffe's Journal (the Queen's modiste) that in 1789 the broad-brimmed hat had entirely displaced the three-cornered hat, and was generally fashionable; also that swords were no longer generally worn.[1]

Vandreuil left the court of France amongst the first party of emigrés after the taking of the Bastille, July, 1789.

The Running Man

Though we were surprised when the second man, also dressed in a large cloak and hat, ran up to us and with extreme earnestness directed us to go to the right rather than to the left, yet we merely thought his manner very French; and as he said in the course of a rather long unintelligible sentence "cherchez la maison," we imagined that he understood that we were

[1] *Modes et Usages*, De Reiset, p. 479, voL i.

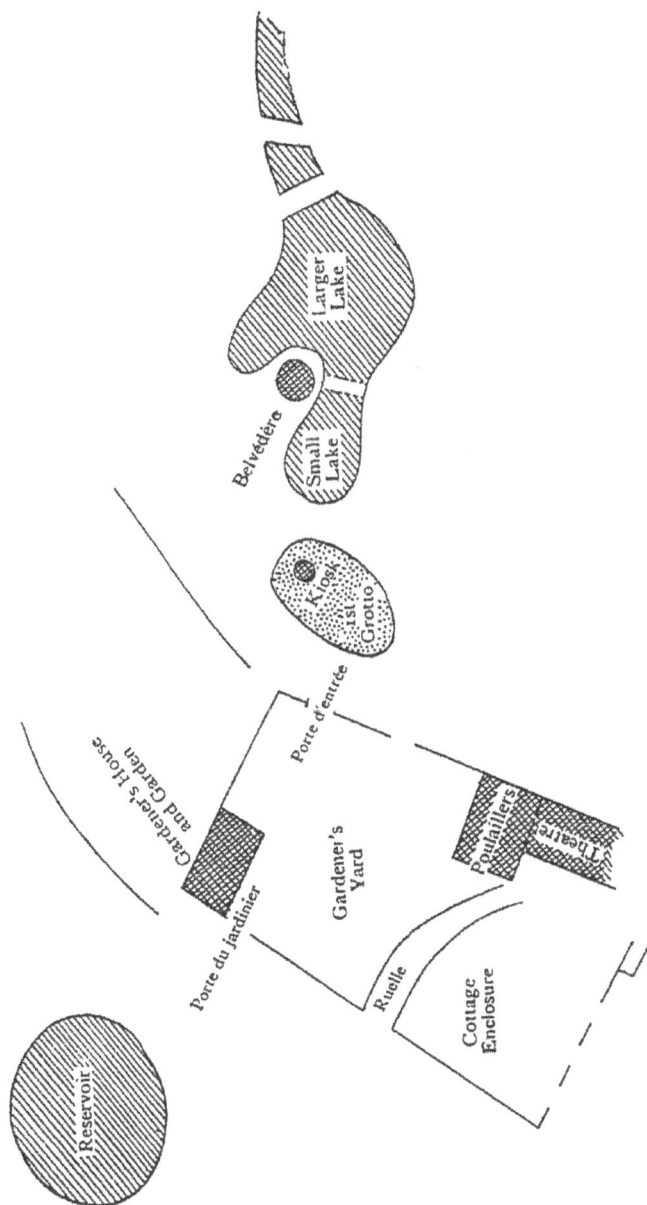

Larger Lake

Belvedere

Small Lake

Kiosk
Isl.
Grotto

Porte d'entrée

Gardener's House
and Garden

Gardener's Yard

Poulaillers

Theatre

Porte du jardinier

Ruelle

Cottage Enclosure

Reservoir

looking for the house, and followed his direction. We noticed that he stood in front of a
rock and seemed to come "either over, round,
or through it."

The following year (1902), we learned that
there was a tradition that on October 5th, 1789,
a messenger was sent to Trianon to warn the
Queen of the approach of the mob from Paris :
that she wished to walk back to the Palace by
the most direct route, but the messenger begged
her to wait at the house whilst he fetched the
carriage, as it was safer to drive back as usual
by the broad roads of the park.

A local tradition affirming this has been
embodied by Madame Julie Lavergne in a
volume entitled (unfortunately for historical
purposes) *Légendes de Trianon*. This particular scene in the story, called " La Dernière
Rose," interested us greatly, for it seemed to
come from an eye-witness and recalled many of
the points of our vision. The Queen, it is said,
had been walking with and talking to Marion
(the daughter of an under-gardener) before
going to her favourite grotto. After remaining
there some time, and on growing alarmed at
her own sad thoughts, the Queen called to

Marion and was surprised to see, instead of the girl, a "garçon de la Chambre" suddenly appear, trembling in all his limbs. After reading the letter brought to her from the Minister at the Palace, the Queen desired him to order the carriage and to let Madame de Tourzel know. The messenger bowed (as our man had done), and once out of sight, ran off at full speed. The Queen followed him to the house.[1]

Enquiries through the publisher, in 1907, as to Madame Lavergne's sources of information, elicited the fact that her informant as to every detail of that scene had been Marion herself. This Marion, the *Légendes* tell us, afterwards married M. Charpentier, an under-gardener, known in 1789 by the name of "Jean de l'Eau," on account of his bringing water daily from Ville d'Avray for the Queen's table. He afterwards became *jardinier en chef*, being appointed in 1805 by Napoleon in succession to Antoine Richard.[2]

The name "Charpantier" appears in 1786 amongst the "ouvriers terrassiers," who clear

[1] *Légendes de Trianon*, p. 75.
[2] *La Belle Jardinière*, Lavergne, pp. 91, 97.

up sticks and leaves, plant flowers, and rake.[1]

In 1783, "Mariamne" received wages for picking up leaves in the Trianon grounds;[2] this is quite possible, as children are said to have been used for that work, and the absence of surname suggests that she was the daughter of one of the gardeners.

The marriage certificate of Alexandre Charpentier, in 1823, gives his father's name as Louis Toussaint Charpentier, and his mother's name as Marie Anne Lemaignan. The marriage certificate of these persons (from which we should have learnt their age) is said to have been destroyed.[3]

In the wages book the names of two "Lemonguin" (elder and younger) appear; also " Magny," but not, so far as has been discovered, Lemaignan.[4] If this Marie Anne Charpentier was 21 years old at her son's birth (November, 1796), she would have been eight years old in 1783, and 14 in 1789. This would suit

[1] *Arch. Nat.* O[1], 1878.   [2] *Arch. Nat.* O[1], 1877.

[3] Letter enclosing marriage ceitificate (copy from the Archives Municipales, Versailles).

[4] *Arch. Nat.* O[1], 1876, 1877.

the "Mariamne" of the Archives, Madame Lavergne's story, and the girl seen by Miss Lamont.

Two more points show the faithfulness of "Marion's" account of that scene. Madame Lavergne (quoting her) says that "pale rays of autumn sunshine lighted up the faded flowers." It must, therefore, have been fairly fine ; and in the wages book it appears that on October 5th, 1789, all the gardeners were at work *in the grounds*, and it is stated that on wet days they worked under cover, sometimes clearing out the passages of the house.[1] Secondly, she says that the Queen sat at the entrance of her grotto, where fallen leaves choked the course of the "ruisseau." From entries of payment it appears that the streams were cleared of dead leaves on October 1st, 2nd, and 3rd, 1789, but not on the 4th or 5th, or ever again.[2] It is exactly a point which Marion would have noticed.

Madame Lavergne lived at Versailles from 1838 till her marriage in 1844, at which time Marion would have been 69 ; and as we believe that Alexandre Charpentier was head gardener

[1] *Ib.* O¹, 1879.   [2] *Ib.* O¹, 1879.

at the Petit Trianon for over fifty years, his
mother would have been easily accessible to
Madame Lavergne during her repeated visits
to Trianon, even after her marriage. Her
father, M. Georges Ozanneaux, was a personal
friend of Louis Philippe, and was constantly
about in the royal palaces.[1]

It is necessary to speak of the grotto; for
Madame Campan says that the Queen "était
assise dans sa grotte . . . lorsqu'elle reçut un
mot d'écrit . . . qui la suppliait de rentrer à
Versailles."[2] Madame Lavergne says "Marion
se dirigea vers le parterre des rosiers, et la
Reine alla s'asseoir à l'entrée de sa grotte
favorite, auprès de la petite source. Les feuilles
jaunies tombées des arbres couvraient la terre
et obstruaient le cours du ruisseau. . . . Le
murmure de la petite cascade qui arrose
l'intérieur de la grotte, retentissait seul dans
le bosquet. . . . Effrayée d'être seule, elle
appela Marion ; mais, au lieu de la jeune fille,
un garçon de la Chambre . . . parut, une lettre
à la main."[3] The Queen cannot, therefore,

[1] *La vie de Madame Lavergne.*
[2] Quoted in *Les Palais de Trianon*, M. de Lescure, p. 148.
[3] *Légendes de Trianon*, Madame Julie Lavergne, p. 75.

have been many steps away from the grotto, at one end or the other, when the messenger came to her.

In 1908 we asked to be shown this grotto, and we were taken to one on the further side of the Belvédère, near the hill called l'Escargot, which was formed in 1781. We felt sure that this could not have been either of the two grottos spoken of in the archives.

In 1777 the end of one grotto is mentioned as being near the *porte d'entrée*, "à la cloison de la porte d'entrée du jardin au bout du grotte trois pottereaux et deux traverses."[1]

In 1777 there was a "projet d'un pont et chutte en rocher, avec parapet." This was probably a bridge (the Vergelay bridge?) over the principal river where it issued from the larger lake. The river was made at this time.[2]

In June, 1780, a new "petite rivière" was planned to receive the water drained from the "ravin de la grotte," and to conduct it into the larger lake. For this purpose a new grotto was made of a "forme ovale, ornée en glaçon," through which the "petite rivière" was to run. A "ravin du petit pont" was also planned.[3]

[1] *Arch. Nat.* O¹, 1875.   [2] *Ib.*   [3] *Ib.*

In August, 1780, masses of rock were procured, and the " petite rivière " was begun, and also a hill was thrown up "pour couvrir la grotte." [1]

In September, 1780, " Bourdin a passé la journée . . . à poser le deuxième pont venant du coté de la grotte." [2] This second bridge was probably the present Rocher bridge, being the second placed over the lakes.   Neither of these two bridges would be the " pont de bois," [3] and " la conduitte en bois," [4] two descriptions of, and identical with, the one alluded to in the words " ravin du petit pont," which was said to have been erected on high ground " au dessus du Rocher du Ravin." [5]

In December, 1780, the work was finished: " Conduitte de l'exécution de la grotte, petite rivière, et chutte d'eau retombante dans le grand lac, autre petits ravins dans la montagne près du grand lac à la fin de la petite rivière de la grotte." [6]

---

[1] *Arch. Nat.* O¹, 1875.   [2] *Ib.*

[3] *Ib.* O¹, 1882. (There was also a " pont de bois à la porte verte " on the east side of the house, *Arch. Nat* O¹, 1881 and 1882.)

[4] *Ib.*   [5] *Ib.* (*Souvenirs d'un Page*, D'Hezecques, p. 242).

[6] *Ib.* 1877.

In 1781 a " montagne " was made " en face du jardin français—en face de la comédie." [1]

In March and April, 1781, a hill called " l'Escargot " was piled up [2]—beyond the Belvédère—and, presumably, a third and very small grotto was made. The creation of the Escargot hill would have made the "ravin" on the north side of the Belvédère, which is still visible, and leads to the greater lake.

There are several reasons why we think that the Queen's grotto (the second made) was on the theatre side of the Belvédère.

1. D'Hezecques' description of it in 1789 shows that, though a " ruisseau " passed through it, persons could go freely out at both ends ; [3] whereas when water was passing down through the upper entrance of the " escargot " grotto, no one could have used it at the same time : there is only room for the water.

2. He speaks of the " prairie " being visible from " une crevasse, qui s'ouvrait à la tête du lit " ; this would have been possible from a grotto on the theatre side, but not on the other, as the " escargot " hill would have been in the way.

[1] *Ib.*   [2] *Ib.*   [3] *Souvenirs d'un Page*, p. 244.

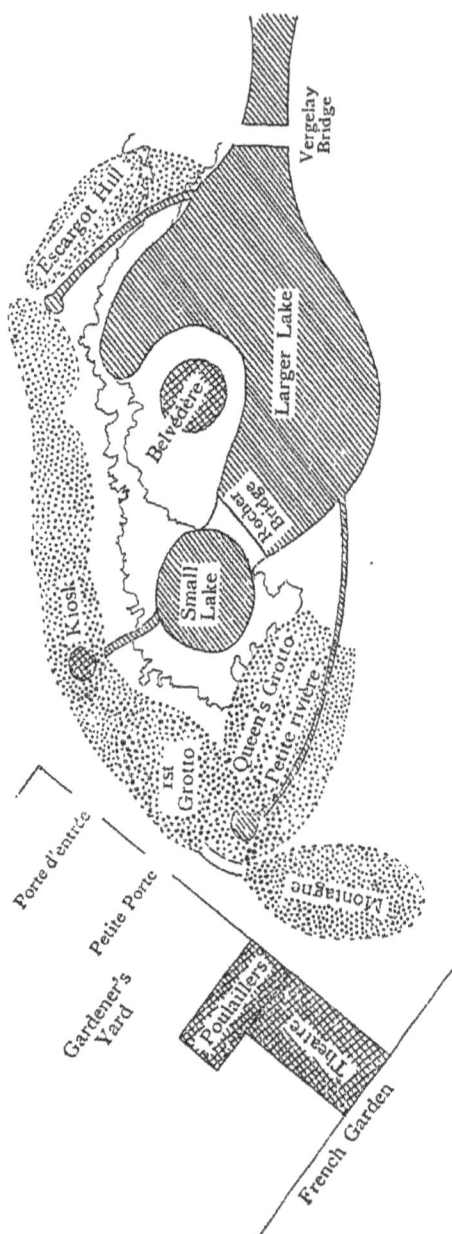

Vergelay Bridge

Escargot Hill

Larger Lake

Belvédère

Riedler Bridge

Small Lake

Kiosk

Queen's Grotto

Petite rivière

1st Grotto

Montagne

Porte d'entrée

Petite Porte

Gardener's Yard

Poulaillers

Théâtre

French Garden

3. D'Hezecques describes a staircase which "conduisait au sommet de la roche," enabling persons to leave hurriedly. There is something like an ancient rock staircase attached to the back of the large rock, giving the name to the Rocher bridge.

4. He says that the grotto was very dark on first entering, and L'Espinasse's picture of the Belvédère in 1783 shows the opening to a cavern on its southern side close to the Rocher bridge,[1] which could be truly described as "venant du coté de la grotte." Could the rock out of which the cavernous mouth was cut have been lifted over the long bridge at some later time? for in L'Espinasse's picture there is no such rock over the bridge as there is now, and the cavern has disappeared.

5. The map of 1783 represents (according to Desjardins) "le projet de Mique complêtement exécuté." In it the figure (5) (indicating the grotto) occurs both at the "escargot" and also on the theatre side of the Belvédère.

In September, 1910, Miss Lamont was asked whether she had seen a map of the place recently placed in the front hall of the Petit

[1] Desjardins, picture, p. 196.

Trianon, and she said No. On going there she found the map, which had not been there at any of her former visits, and saw that the grottos were put, as far as she could judge, just where we had long ago, through elaborate personal research, decided must be their real position. She could only make this out by standing on the table amongst the books and photographs, the map being hung too high to be easily seen.

Several further points of interest have emerged in connection with the running man.

1. In April, 1908, we learned that our being directed at all in the grounds was unusual, for since September, 1870, they have been thrown open until dark. The difficulty now experienced is to find a guide.

2. He spoke of the "maison." In 1907 we found out that the Queen was in the habit of calling the Petit Trianon "ma maison de Trianon," to distinguish it from the Palace and the Chateau.[1] Louis XVI. had presented it to Marie Antoinette on his accession.

[1] Desjardins, pp. 103, 73.

3. The Queen is reported by Marion to have addressed the messenger as " Breton."[1]   This was not an uncommon name about the court and old Versailles.   The court almanack for 1783 shows that then the Queen had a Page " de l'Écurie," called "De Bretagne." (The Pages de la Chambre sometimes became " de l'Écurie" before receiving a commission or some other office.[2])   He is not mentioned in the almanack of 1789, but (as we know from other instances) it does not follow necessarily that he had no office in the household.   Madame Éloffe (the Queen's modiste) mentions a Mademoiselle Breton amongst the Queen's women, who does not appear in the almanack.[3]

If " De Bretagne " was 16 years old in 1783, he would have been 22 in 1789,—just in the fresh young vigour suitable to our running man.

The name " Breton " may have referred to his nationality only, for in November, 1907, we discovered that the accent in which the man spoke to us resembled the Breton accent,

[1] *Légendes de Trianon*, p. 75.
[2] *Souvenirs d'un Page*, pp. 112, 118.
[3] *Modes et Usages*, De Reiset, vol. i. p. 445.

in which the consonants are strengthened and the diphthongs broadened.

In the autumn of 1909 we read the Baron de Frénilly's *Souvenirs*, in which it is stated that wigs were universally worn by gentlemen in French society up till 1787. After that date powdered hair became the general usage; the first person (M. de Valence) who ventured to appear with unpowdered hair did so, apparently, in 1788, after which it became a mark of extreme fashion.[1]

The same was the case with buckled shoes. Gold, silver, stones, and rosettes had been required for a gentleman's dress ornaments; but after the commercial treaty with England in 1786, steel was used for everything. Buckled shoes are expressly mentioned as being very fashionable in 1789, and there was, at that time, a rage for steel ornaments.[2]

Bridge over Little Cascade

Following the man's direction, we turned to the right and walked over a small rustic bridge which crossed a tiny waterfall coming from

[1] *Souvenirs du Baron de Frénilly*, p. 80.   [2] *Ib.* p. 80.

above us, on our right hand, and flowing in
front of a little rocky cliff with ferns growing in
the crevices.   The water seemed to have formed
a steep narrow little ravine, which shelved away
below us to a little glimmering pool.

Neither bridge, nor cascade, nor ravine can
be found, or anything suggesting them.   In
1905 the person in charge at the house assured
Miss Lamont that there never had been more
than one cascade, meaning the rush of water
under the Rocher bridge.   The Rocher bridge
is certainly not the one we crossed, which was
high above the level of the lakes.

In 1907 we bought *Souvenirs d'un Page* by
the Comte D'Hezecques.   He says : " En face
du chateau, une pelouse . . . se terminait par
une roche ombragée de pins, de thuyas, de
mélèzes,   et   *surmontée d'un pont rustique,*
comme on en rencontre dans les montagnes de
la Suisse et les précipices du Valais.   Cette
perspective agreste et sauvage rendait plus
douce celle . . . de la troisième façade du
chateau.[1]

He also speaks of water passing through the
moss-lined grotto, which, according to our idea,

[1] *Souvenirs d'un Page*, p. 242.

must have been below us, but close by on our right hand.[1] Madame Lavergne writes of the "petite cascade" and of the sound of it in the grotto.[2]

In April, 1908, extracts from Mique's accounts and plans for the Trianon grounds were procured from the archives, giving the history of the grottos. "Juin 4, 1780, fait un model en terre *du ravin du petit pont*."[3] "1788, Pièce au dessus du *Rocher du Ravin* et . . . passage des voitures sur *le pont de bois* . . . Pièce à droite *en face du Rocher du Ravin*."[4] "Au long du chemin de l'emplacement de la Ruine *sur la conduitte en bois à la deuxième source du Ravin*."[5] The first source was probably close to the "Ruine" (our kiosk?). The second "source" might coincide with Desjardins' "source," which he places a few steps from the *poulaillers*,[6] and was probably meant to feed the "petite rivière," which passed through the Queen's grotto, carrying off the water from the stagnant pool between the grottos to the larger lake.[7] That would exactly agree with the

[1] *Souvenirs d'un Page*, p. 243. [2] *La Dernière Rose*, p. 75.
[3] *Arch. Nat.* O^I, 1875. [4] *Ib.* O^I, 1882.
[5] *Ib.* O^I, 1882. [6] *Le Petit Trianon*, p. 90.
[7] *Arch Nat.* O^I, 1875.

position of our little cascade, small bridge, and glimmering pool.

In April, 1908, an old MS. map was found amongst such archive papers as relate to the grottos, showing a small bridge in the right position relatively to the lakes, the Rocher bridge, and the place where we believe the Queen's grotto to have been.

Isolated Rock

In 1908 we found a mass of rocks standing in the dry bed of the small lake.   On one rock covered with ivy were two full-grown pine trees.   It seems unlikely that the trees should have originally been in the small circular basin of water.

D'Hezecques says that thuya and pine trees were planted high up over the grotto to give it the appearance of a Swiss mountain.[1]   The grotto was destroyed about 1792, and it is possible that some of the rocks covering it were displaced and allowed to slip into the lake below, and that the present pine trees may have been seedlings at the time, for we are

[1] *Souvenirs d'un Page*, p. 242.

told that the life of a pine tree is from 100 to 200 years old.

In 1908 we noticed that at one side of this ivy-covered rock were peculiar projections; one of these was broken off short, but the other was intact. We thought they might once have formed supports for a small bridge.

Rocks are said to have been placed in 1788 at the "montagne des Pins à gauche et en montant au Rocher." "Montagne des Pins à droite en montant au Rocher."[1]

In January, 1791, trees were torn up from the montagnes.

In February, March, April, 1792, every few days occurs the entry: "Journée à arracher les Thuja sur les montagnes.[2]

According to the old picture by L'Espinasse (1783), there was nothing over the low long bridge between the two lakes, but there was by the side of it, just where the grotto would have ended, a cavern in a rock.[3] This is no longer there; but possibly the face of rock with the cavern-like opening may have been lifted over the bridge, and account for the very peculiar

[1] *Arch. Nat.* O[1], 1882.　　　[2] *Ib.* O[1], 1879.
[3] Desjardins, p. 196.

rock which is at present above the bridge, causing it to be called the Rocher bridge. A rough rock staircase which has no meaning is attached to this rock behind. D'Hezecques speaks of a staircase as having been within the grotto leading up to its entrance on the high ground on the montagnes—has it been moved to the lower end of the grotto?

There is now no isolated rock standing up as we saw it behind the running man;—only mounds covered with shrubs and trees. But in the archives there is a note saying that in 1788 rocks were placed in various parts, and one is especially mentioned, " pièce donnant au bord du lac de l'ancien côté des rochers . . . *au long du chemin de l'emplacement de la Ruine sur la conduitte en bois à la deuxième source du Ravin.*"[1] This would have been the path we were on in 1901.

Pelouse

It is easy to suppose that between the years 1901-4 trees were cleared away from the rough ground on the north side of the house, which in

[1] *Arch. Nat.* O[1], 1882.

1901 had given it the look of an orchard. So much was this the case that the lady sitting under the north terrace was thought to be making a study of tree stems; for she was looking into trees, and she held a large paper in her hand, and, as we passed, held it out at arm's length.

At present there are trees on each side of the pelouse, and one growing near the site of the old Jeu de Bague, but none growing in front of the house, and it all looks drier, brighter, and less confined than in 1901.

We have found two interesting mentions of this *pelouse*.

Before the new theatre was built in 1779, the old *comédie* stood on it for three years. When the *comédie* was moved it gave place to a "pelouse parsemée d'arbres."[1]

The Lady

Nothing unusual marked the lady sitting on a low seat on the grass immediately under the north terrace. I remember recognising that

[1] Desjardins, pp. 107, 120; *Arch. Nat.* O¹, 1875, 1877; Terrade, *Le Théâtre de la Reine*, p. 23.

her light-coloured skirt, white fichu, and straw hat were in the present fashion, but they struck me as rather dowdy in the general effect. She was so near us that I looked full at her, and she bent slightly forward to do the same.

I never doubted that we had both seen her, and three months after was astonished to hear that Miss Lamont had not done so. That sounds simple to others, to ourselves it is inexplicable. Miss Lamont had seen the plough, the cottage, the woman, and the girl, which I had not; but she is generally more observant than I, and there were other things to look at. At this moment there was nothing to see on the right, and merely a shady, damp-looking meadow on the left, and the lady was sitting in front of the house we had come to see, and were both eagerly studying. The lady was visible some way off; we walked side by side straight up to her, leaving her slightly on the left hand as we passed up the steps to the terrace, from whence I saw her again from behind, and noticed that her fichu had become a pale green.

The fact that she had not been seen at a moment when we were both a little exercised by our meeting with the men,—one looking so unpleasant, and the other so unaccountably and infectiously excited,—made a deep impression.

The legend that we heard the following winter of the Queen having been occasionally seen sitting in front of the house in the English garden, is of course incapable of proof; but three things were to us full of interest.

I. In 1902 I saw Wertmüller's picture of the Queen, which alone of all the many portraits shown me in any way brought back the face I had seen; for the face was more square and the nose shorter. A few weeks later we read that Madame Campan considered it almost the only picture of her that was really like, though other people thought that it did not do her justice.

II. In April, 1908, we learned that there was only one time during the Queen's tenure of the Petit Trianon when she could have seen strangers in her gardens, from which, in earlier days, the Court was entirely excluded, and to which even the King only came by invitation. For four months, after May, 1789, when the Court was carried off to Paris, the public streamed in as it liked. So many came to see the place that had been too much talked about,

that the King and Queen had gone that summer to Marly for a little rest and quiet. That
was the time when D'Hezecques, with one
of the deputies, walked round and saw the
grotto and the little bridge. At the time
the Trianon officials must have learnt to treat
strangers with cold politeness, but probably
resenting the necessity. This exactly accounts
for the manner of the guards at the *porte du
jardinier*; they made no difficulty, and told us
that we should find the house by going that
way, but in quite an unusual manner for
Frenchmen. It was mechanical and disen-
gaged.

III. In the summer of 1908 we read the Journal of Madame Éloffe (the Queen's modiste).
She says that during the year 1789 the Queen
was extremely economical, and had very few
dresses made. Madame Éloffe repaired several
light, washing, short skirts, and made, in July
and September, two green silk bodices, besides
many large white fichus. This agrees exactly
with the dress seen in 1901. The skirt was not
of a fresh white, but was light coloured,—slightly
yellowish. The white fichu in front seemed to
have an edge of green or gold, just as it would

have appeared if the white muslin, or gauze, was over green. The colour would have shown more clearly at the back, but in front, where the white folds accumulated, the green would have been less prominent. The straight edge in front and the frill behind had often puzzled me, but in Madame Éloffe's illustrations of the fashions at that time there are instances of the same thing. There is in the book a coloured picture of the green silk bodice, with all the measurements to enable her to fit the Queen perfectly.[1]

Jeu de Bague

As we approached the terrace at the north-west corner of the house, we had some barrier on our right hand entirely blocking the view, so that we could see nothing but the meadow on our left hand, and the house with its terrace in front.

At present the pathway which curves towards the house, and is very likely the old one, has a large bare space on the right hand with one beautiful old tree growing on the edge of it;

[1] *Modes et Usages*, De Reiset, vol. i. pp. 479, 404, 423, 365, 369.

and from some way off one can easily see across it to the chapel beyond the French garden.   A long piece of wall extends westward from the terrace, round which one has to go into the French garden in order to find the staircase; whilst the whole length of wall, including part of the north terrace, is hidden by a large old spreading bush, completely covering the place where the lady sat.

Originally, we could not see the steps whilst on the path, but after we had passed the barrier on our right hand we found them at once without going round any wall.

The map of 1783 shows us that the Jeu de Bague (put up in 1776) once stood on what is now bare space.   It was a circular building surrounded by a wooden gallery, masked by trees.   This would have completely shut out the view, and the path was probably curved on its account.

In 1907, we learnt that the Queen had a passage made under the terrace from the house to the Jeu de Bague; and in 1908 we discovered the old walled-up doorway leading into the English garden behind the bush.   The ground seems to have been a good deal raised since it was used. Four feet to the right of this door, just at the point where the top of the present staircase is reached, is a change of masonry, the rest of the wall being plastered over.

In 1910 we found that this extension of the wall was composed of rubble. Perhaps it had been added to the stone terrace in the time of Louis Philippe. If the present staircase is old, we could have reached it easily from the English garden in the absence of the wall, but if it is not old, and it is not indicated in Mique's map, there may have been something quite different—even steps turned northward towards the English garden.

In 1910 we also learned that the bush had been planted when the Duchesse d'Orleans occupied the house.

The Chapel Man

Whilst we were standing at the south-west end of the terrace above the French garden, the door of a building at right angles to the house suddenly opened, and a young man came out and slammed the door behind him. He came to

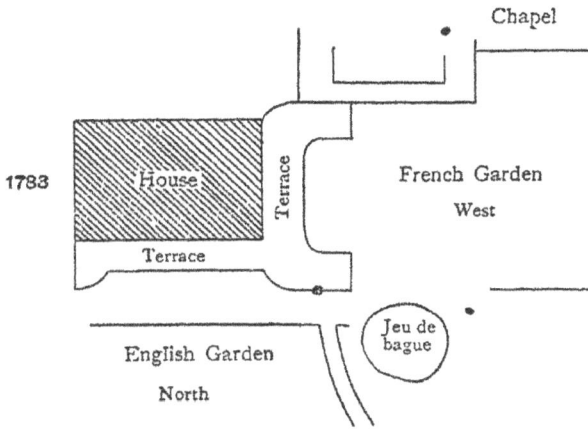

1783

Chapel

House

Terrace

French Garden

West

Terrace

English Garden

North

Jeu de bague

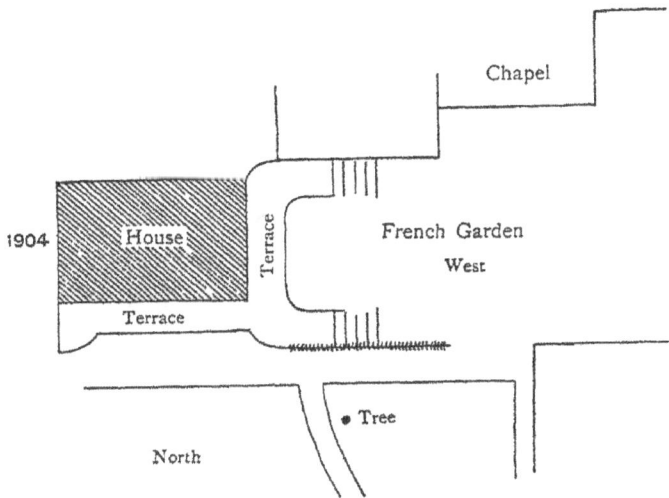

1904

Chapel

House

Terrace

French Garden

West

Terrace

North

Tree

us very quickly along a level. His manner was
jaunty and imperious, and he told us that the
only way to the house was by the *cour d'honneur*. It was difficult to hear what he said.
We thought at once that we were trespassing
and looked for some way down from the terrace,
upon which he constituted himself our guide,
and with an inquisitive, amused expression,
went with us a little way down the French
garden, and showed us out into the avenue by
a broad road.

There is much to say about this incident.

I. The man evidently did not mean us to
stand on the terrace so near to the house, and
forced us to move away. He was the second
person that afternoon who had excitedly insisted
on our going one way rather than another; but
now we know that since 1870 the gardens and
terraces have been made public until dark, and
people walk about freely. No one has ever
stopped us since, nor can we hear of anyone
else who has been guided as we were.

II. In 1905 we found that the building out
of which the man came was the old chapel,
which is in a ruinous condition.

In 1906, Miss Lamont had leave to go into the

chapel, which she had to enter from the avenue, there being no entrance from the garden. When inside she saw that the door out of which he had come was one leading into the royal gallery. The gallery now stands isolated high up on the north wall of the chapel. Formerly, from inside, it was reached by a door on a landing at the top of a staircase. This staircase is completely broken down, and the floor of the landing is gone, so that there is now no access to the gallery. The terrace door of the gallery is bolted, barred, and cobwebbed over from age and disuse. The guide said that the door had not been opened in the memory of any man there: not since it was used by the Court.

In April, 1907, Miss Lamont went again to the chapel, this time with two companions. Their guide then told them that the doors had not been opened to his knowledge for fifteen years, and the great door not since it was used by the court of Louis XVI. "Moi, je suis ici depuis quinze ans, et je sais que les portes ont été condamnées bien avant cela." He added that having the sole charge of the keys, no one could have opened the doors without his know-

F

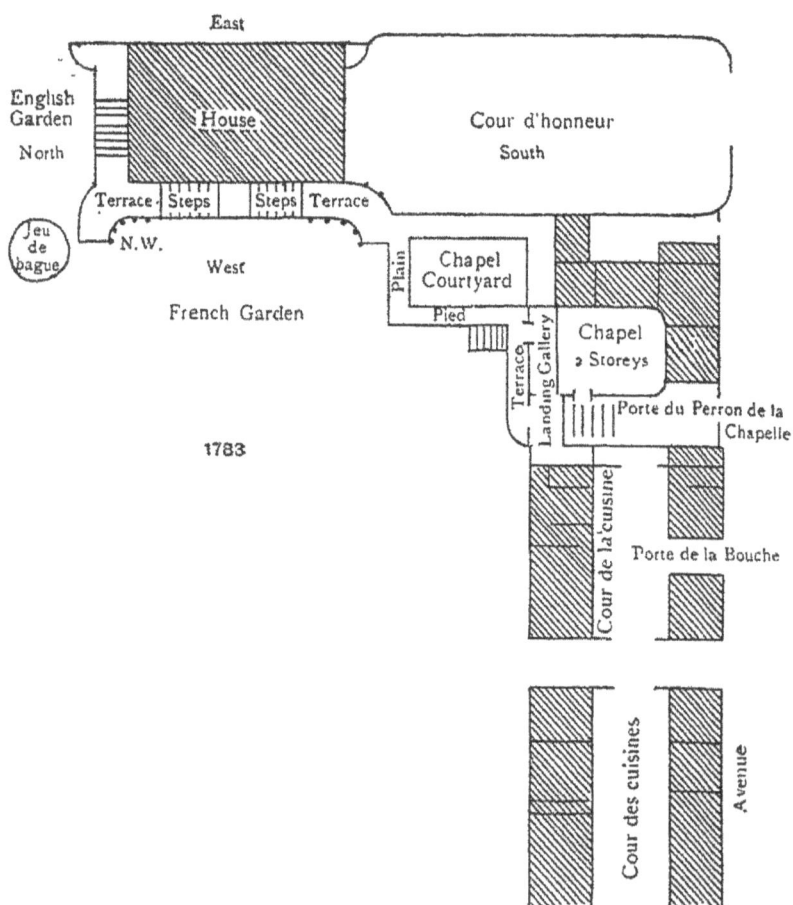

East

English Garden

North

House

Cour d'honneur

South

Terrace Steps Steps Terrace

Jeu de bague

N.W.

West

French Garden

Plain

Chapel Courtyard

Pied

Terrace

Landing Gallery

Chapel 2 Storeys

Porte du Perron de la Chapelle

1783

Cour de la cuisine

Porte de la Bouche

Cour des cuisines

Avenue

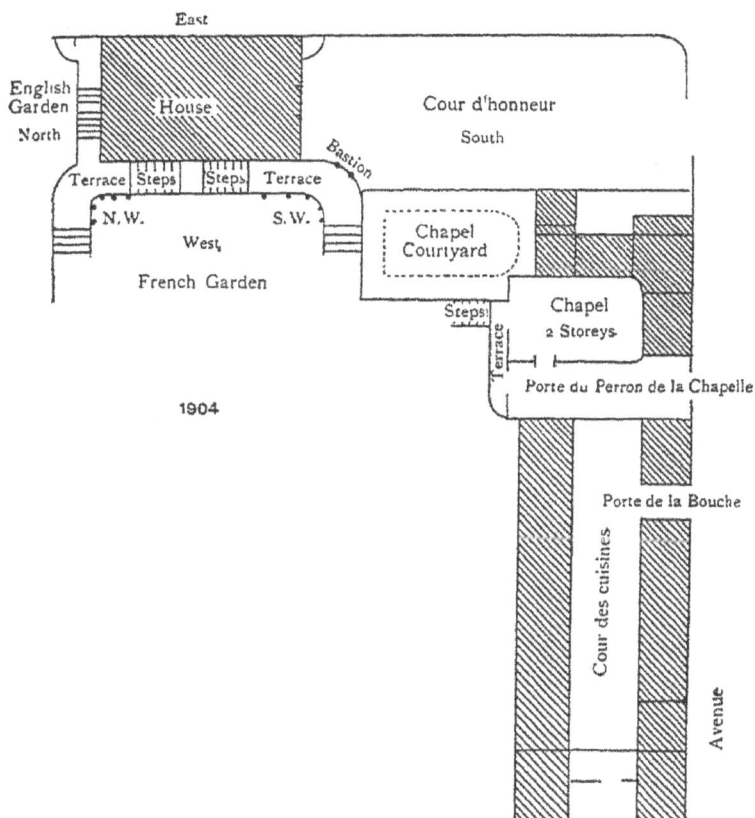

East

English
Garden

North

House

Cour d'honneur

South

Bastion

Terrace | Steps | Steps | Terrace

N.W.   S.W.

West

French Garden

Chapel
Courtyard

Steps

Terrace

Chapel
2 Storeys

Porte du Perron de la Chapelle

1904

Porte de la Bouche

Terrace

Cour des cuisines

Avenue

ledge, and smiled at the idea as he looked at the blocked-up old doors.

In August, 1907, two other friends went to the chapel and entirely confirmed all that had been said about its ruined condition and the impossibility of the great door having been opened in 1901. Their guide told them that the big door had been Marie Antoinette's private entrance. The gallery was still standing and had two chairs on it of gilt and old red velvet; but when they asked whether it was possible to enter it, the guide laughed and pointed to the staircase. There was no other entrance, he said, and the stairs had been in that condition for the last ten years. They thought from the look of the stairs that they had probably been so for much longer.

In September, 1910, a fifth friend went to the chapel and bore witness to the impossibility of the doors having been used in 1901, and was told that the staircase had finally broken down fifteen years before.

III. From Desjardins' book we learned that the Queen's concierge had been Bonnefoy du Plan. He had rooms between the chapel and the *cour d'honneur* and kept his stores in a loft over the chapel, reached by the now broken-down old staircase. The window of this attic still looks over the French garden, and from it, in old days, he would have seen anyone approaching the house from that side. The name of the *suisse* (the porter) in charge of the *porte du perron de la chapelle* in 1789 was Lagrange. His rooms were immediately behind the chapel, looking into the avenue.[1] He could easily have been sent through the chapel to interview strangers on the terrace.

IV. We did not lose sight of the man when he came to us. As it is now he must have gone quite out of sight, down one flight of steps outside the chapel door, and (after passing under a high wall) have reached the terrace (where we were standing) by a second set of steps. The present wall of the chapel court-yard is so high as to hide half the door, and a large chestnut tree in the courtyard hides it from the part of the terrace on which we were,—even in winter.

In April, 1907, we discovered that a continuous ground-floor passage from the kitchens once passed the chapel door to the house.

[1] Desjardins', *Le Petit Trianon*, pp. 188, 189.

This set us wondering as to whether there had ever been a pathway above it. The same year we were told that the chapel courtyard round which the passage had gone had been enlarged.

In August, 1907, two friends reported to us and photographed a mark on the outside of the courtyard wall, showing where it might at some time have been raised.

In March, 1908, another mark on the chapel was discovered, revealing that there had once been an inner wall to the courtyard, which might have been removed when the courtyard was enlarged. We also found out that the levels were so different that the passage would have been partly underground on the side of the French garden, but in the rez de chaussée in the courtyard and where it flanked the cour d'honneur. We noticed from the photographs that the bastion at the south-west corner of the house in the cour d'honneur looked older than the top part of the wall adjoining it above the chapel courtyard.

In September, 1910, permission was given to enter this courtyard; when within, it was definitely explained that above the kitchen passage there had been a covered way, by which the Queen could enter the chapel from the house in wet weather. The top of this covered way had been " de plain pied," joining the bit of terrace outside the chapel door to the terrace by the house. This would have been the level way along which our man came to us.

The marks of the passage and covered way (forming the intervening piece of terrace) were perfectly clear both on the inside of the present wall and on the ground in the courtyard. The present balustrade adjoining the bastion was probably placed when the old covered way was destroyed and the outside wall was raised. It was also noticed that the round windows in the bastion lighted the lower kitchen passage ; but that those facing the French garden, being on a higher level, lighted the covered way.

The guide stated that the tree in the centre of the chapel courtyard had certainly been planted after the days of the monarchy.

V. The road from the garden to the avenue (through which the man ushered us) was not far from the chapel, and was broad enough to

admit a coach. The present one is narrower
and further to the west.

In 1907, we read a note by M. de Nolhac in
Les Consignes de Marie Antoinette in which he
says that the old *porte de la ménagerie* which
must have led from the avenue to the French
garden is now lost, but that it must have been
"tout auprès des bâtiments de la Conciergerie
et des cuisines."[1] We thought that perhaps it
was the one we went by, and on looking at
Mique's map of 1783 found a broad road
dividing the kitchen court into two parts.
At present solid continuous buildings on the
two sides of the kitchen court show no sign of
an entrance, though in two places the roofs
have a difference of level.

In April, 1909, a Frenchman, who sold prints
and seemed to be a specialist in maps, said that
Mique's map was the only authoritative one.

In September, 1910, we learned from the
first authority that Mique's map was "exact":
that the road found in it had certainly existed,
and its position relatively to the pond in the
French garden was explained. A search for
some sign of it was at once made, and success·

[1] page 7.

fully.   On the garden side, not at all far from
the chapel, the jamb of an old opening still
projects from the building, covered with ivy ;
and the stones on the ground are laid, for a
space of about twelve paces, the other way
from the stones on either side, evidently to
make a carriage road.   A large rectangular
stone was lying on the ground which might
either have been a step, or part of the second
jamb.   On the avenue side marks of an opening of some sort can be traced through the
plaster with which Louis Philippe finished the
buildings after restoring and also altering them.
The opening would have included two present
windows not far from the *porte de la bouche*, as
the signs of it are visible on both sides of the
opening, and the space between is from twelve
to twenty paces.

Within the kitchen court the buildings have
been so altered and plastered over that no
traces of change could be found.

All the points corresponded with the recollection of the roadway through which we had
passed in 1901.

Two Labourers with Cart

On her second visit, January 2nd, 1902, Miss Lamont saw, in the field near the Hameau, two labourers, in brown tunics and bright-coloured short capes, loading a cart with sticks. The capes hardly came below their shoulders and had hoods : one was bright blue and the other red.

In May, 1904, a search was made in the archives with the result that it was clear that carts and horses for the purpose of tidying the grounds were hired by the day in old times, and not kept in the farm for constant use. In January, 1789, two men, instead of the usual one ("plus un homme"), were hired " pour ramasser les loques des chenilles et les brûler."[1]

In 1906 we discovered that the tunic and short cape were worn by the bourgeoisie in the fourteenth century.

In April, 1908, we had proof that the artisans were wearing them in the eighteenth century, and that some of the working men at Trianon in 1776 had "hardes de couleur."[2]

[1] *Arch. Nat.* O¹, 1879.   [2] *Ibid.* O¹, 1877.

The entry in the wages book showed that up to 1783, from time to time "une voiture à cheval, et un conducteur," were hired for picking up branches and sticks in the parks: but on *October 4th, 1789,* a cart with two horses (almost certainly requiring two men) was hired *for three days* for the purpose.[1]

In August, 1908, a former gardener, who had been at Trianon long enough to remember both the Charpentiers, father and son, laughed at the idea of such a dress being worn now at Trianon, as it belonged to the "ancien régime." He assured us that carts of the present day in France had scarcely altered at all in type, and that the two now in use at Trianon (which we found in a shed at the *ferme*) were of the old pattern.

The Wood

Miss Lamont then went from the Hameau towards the small Orangerie. Whilst on the ascending path she saw, on looking back, a man passing in front of, or in, a distant plantation on his way to the Hameau. He

Ibid. O¹, 1879.

was dressed in the cloak and hat we had seen the previous summer.

She then descended to the low ground in front of the Belvédère and crossed one of the bridges over the principal river (not the Rocher bridge, but possibly the Vergelay bridge). After going forward a little she turned, meaning to go back to the Hameau, and recrossed either the same bridge, or the next one which is very near the Vergelay. She immediately found herself in a wood of very tall trees, with such high, thick under-growth that (even though it was winter) she could not see through it. Well-kept paths opened at intervals right and left at different angles, and they gave the impression of being so arranged as to lead round and round. She had the feeling of being in the midst of crowds passing and repassing her, and heard voices and sounds of dresses. On looking back she found the view as completely blocked as it was in front and to the sides. After vainly pursuing the confusing paths for some time, she found herself close to the hill leading to the Orangerie.

In 1904 and in 1908 we tried to find this

wood, without results.   There are open plantations, but they have no undergrowths concealing
paths from one another, even in summer.
Several people have gone independently to
look for the wood, but have not found it.

In 1905 Miss Lamont was told by the chief
authority that in this direction trees had been
thinned and not replaced.

The entries in the archives indicate that
there must have been woods near by in
which paths were cut for the Queen; it is
also likely that the older woods, such as
Les Onze Arpents, are not referred to; for
when these plantations were made thousands
of lower shrubs were bought to be placed
under the trees, which were paid for by the
King.[1] In the gardeners' wages book, the
gathering up and occasional burnings of
undergrowths in a wood (apparently in this
part of the garden) are alluded to.[2]

In Mique's map (1783) the wood with its
diverging paths can be plainly seen. It is
approached by the two bridges over the
river, and stretches towards the hill on
which the Orangerie stands.

[1] *Arch. Nat.* O¹, 1876.   [2] *Ibid.* O¹, 1877.

The Music

Whilst in the wood Miss Lamont heard sounds of a band of violins drifting past her from the direction of the house. The sounds were very soft and intermittent, and were lower in pitch than bands of to-day. She could afterwards write down from memory about twelve bars, but without all the inner harmonies.

She ascertained immediately afterwards that no band had been playing out of doors that afternoon at Versailles. It was a cold, wet winter's afternoon.

In March, 1907, the twelve bars were shown to a musical expert, who said (without having heard the story) that the bars could hardly belong to one another, but that the idiom dated from about 1780. He found a grammatical mistake in one bar. After hearing the story, he said that bands in the eighteenth century were lower in pitch than they are now. He suggested the name of Sacchini.

In March, 1908, Miss Lamont and a friend

were told in Versailles that no bands had been allowed to play in the park in winter until 1907. They also ascertained that no music played at Versailles, or in the park, could have been heard at Trianon.

In the same month they searched through a great deal of unpublished music in the Conservatoire de Musique at Paris, and discovered that the twelve bars represented the chief motives of the light opera of the eighteenth century, excluding Rameau and his school, and that, as far as they could discover, nothing like them occurred in the opera of 1815 onward. They were found in Sacchini, Philidor, Monsigny, Grétry, and Pergolesi. Grammatical mistakes were found in Monsigny and Grétry.

Sacchini.

" Dardanus." General likeness.

"Œdipe à Colone." Number 6. Two bars intact in the key answering to that heard in 1902, allowing for the rise of a semi-tone, which had taken place since the eighteenth century. This was proved by later editions of operatic music, in which the songs were dropped a semi-tone to retain the original key.

Philidor in a collection of single airs (Rigaudons, 1767)—the cadence.

"Le Maréchal Ferrand": repetition of single notes, the first bar of the melody, and many other hints of likeness.

Duni. 1765. The same general characteristics, but no exact resemblance.

Monsigny.

"Le Roi et le Fermier." Written for performance at the opening of the new theatre at the Petit Trianon, August 1, 1780, when the Queen first acted herself. Up to 1908 it had not been republished. In it the figure of the first of the twelve bars was found.

"Le Déserteur." No published edition was found after 1830. In one published before that date the last three bars of the music were found, and the melody of the first bars was assigned to the second violins, and very freely, in inversions and variations, in other places. The character of the accompaniment was reminding.

Thirds and sixths constantly occur in Monsigny's music.

Grétry. The same phrases were used and the ascending passage was found. Also, hidden consecutive fifths.

Pergolesi.

" Largo and Andante in D." Similar phrases were used.

The Tall Gardener

Miss Lamont then went along the upper path, and when between the Escargot hill and the Belvédère, she met a very tall gardener of apparently great strength, with long muscular arms. She thought that with his long hair and grizzled, untidy beard and general appearance, he had the look of an Englishman rather than a Frenchman.

He was dressed in a rough knitted jersey, and a small dark blue round cap was set at the back of his head. She enquired where

G

she should find the Queen's grotto, and he walked a little way beside her to show her the way.

Miss Lamont expected to have to turn back to the present grotto, and when she remarked that they were going past the Belvédère, he replied firmly that they *must* go past the Belvédère, and said that it was necessary to have been born and bred in the place to know the way so that " personne ne pourrait vous tromper."

It appears that from 1870 onwards the gardeners at Trianon have been selected from the technical schools, and that it is now a matter of competition, no one being appointed simply because he was born and bred there. We do not know whether this is the case with the under-gardeners ; nor whether the tall gardener was a chief official or not.

In August, 1908, we were told by a former gardener that their dress now is the same as the traditional dress of the ancien régime, viz., a rough knitted jersey with a small *casquette* on the head.

In the old weekly wages book there appears, for several years, the name " l'Anglais "—probably a nickname.[1]   He must not be confused with John Egleton, who remained at Trianon only a few months, and whose wages were settled on his departure by a bill which is still in existence, but is not in the wages book.[2]

We owe our researches as to the position of the Queen's grotto almost entirely to the tall gardener's decided directions and guidance to the part of the English garden between the Belvédère and the *montagnes* close to the theatre.

E. M.

F. L.

September, 1910.

---

[1] *Arch. Nat.* O[I], 1877.   [2] *Ib.* O[I], 1880.

CHAPTER III

ANSWERS TO QUESTIONS WHICH WE HAVE BEEN ASKED

1. One of us has to own to having powers of second sight, etc., deliberately undeveloped, and there are psychical gifts in her family. She comes of a Huguenot stock. The other is one of a large and cheerful party, being the seventh daughter and of a seventh son; her mother and grandmother were entirely Scotch, and both possessed powers of premonition accompanied by vision. Her family has always been sensitive to ghost stories in general, but mercilessly critical of particular ones of a certain type.

2. Both of us have inherited a horror of all forms of occultism. We lose no opportunity of preaching against them as unwholesome and

misleading; because they mostly deal with conditions of physical excitement, and study of the abnormal and diseased, including problems of disintegrated personality which present such close analogy to those of insanity. We have the deepest distrust in, and distaste for, stories of abnormal appearances and conditions. We find narratives of *revenants* unconvincing, and studiously avoid (as utterly lowering) all spiritualistic methods of communication with the dead. We have never had the curiosity, or the desire, to help in the investigations of psychical phenomena.

3. We belong to no new schools of thought : we are the daughters of English clergymen, and heartily hold and teach the faith of our fathers.

4. We are quite certain that neither of us exerted any conscious influence over the other ; for though we saw much in common, yet each had independent vision. We should think it wrong either to exercise, or to submit to, influence of that nature. We are independent people and accustomed to stand on our own feet.

5. Our condition at the time was one of

perfect health and enjoyment of a holiday in the midst of very hard work.

6. We were entirely ignorant of the history and traditions of the place, and continued our conversation about other things after every interruption. We did not even know that we were in the grounds of the Petit Trianon until we saw the house.

7. At the time Miss Lamont thought that there was something unusual about the place and was puzzled ; the same idea returned to her occasionally during the following week. Miss Morison put her feeling of oppression down to some physical fatigue in herself, and so said nothing ; for we did not know one another very well at that time, were in the relation of hostess and guest, and neither of us thought of enlarging on uncomfortable sensations. After some days, when Miss Morison was writing an account of the expedition, she thought it over with care, and realised that her sensations had not been caused by fatigue, but had produced fatigue. She became convinced that the oppression had been due to some unusual cause in the place itself, and instantly turned to Miss Lamont and said so. Miss Lamont agreed.

We then discussed the man by the kiosk and the running man, but said that there was much besides which had caused dreamy depression. Miss Morison returned to her letter and wrote down : " We both think that the Petit Trianon is haunted."

When we met next (three months later) we talked it over again, and finding that Miss Lamont had not seen the lady, and that Miss Morison had not seen the plough, cottage, woman, or girl, we resolved to write separate accounts of our visit in order to find the discrepancies, but with no idea of making exhaustive histories. These papers are still in existence. Miss Lamont, in her story, used the words " uncanny " and " eerie " to describe her feelings, but they did not mean that she had the least idea at the time that any of the people encountered were unreal or ghostly ; this was still more true of the scenery.

8. During the next three years, Miss Lamont repeatedly took parties of girls over the Trianon, and she reported that the place was changed ; but Miss Morison could not believe it, and even made maps to remind her what their old route had been. After Miss Morison had paid a

second visit to Trianon in July, 1904, and had
found out for herself that the place was entirely
changed, it was resolved to undertake a personal
research into the matter, and to say no more
until we had discovered for ourselves whether
our vivid recollections of the people and
the place tallied with any ancient reality or
not.

Up to that time we had told the story freely,
with the result that we have constantly traced
it inaccurately reported in histories, sometimes
purporting to have come from other sources,
and even in newspapers and small periodicals.
After research had begun to yield interesting
results, we were obliged to be silent, finding that publicity prevented our getting at
evidence.

We are very busy people, and have refused
to let the incident take a prominent place in our
time, interests, or fancy, though from the first
we agreed to lose no given opportunity of
elucidation. The evidence has, therefore, come
slowly ; but the manner in which it has come
has often been a source of surprise. If a helpful
person came in our way, we showed the whole
thing : if we were casually asked if certain

reports were true, we confirmed them (when we could), but said nothing further. We were anxious to wait until we had exhausted every possible means of satisfying ourselves as to the exact amount of interest attaching to the story; and it was several years before we had to believe that we had seen the place as it had been a hundred years before, and as it had not been, in several important particulars, since 1835. The research had been undertaken with the idea of *disproving* the suggestion that anything unusual had happened, for we were resolved not to deceive ourselves or anyone else, if personal industry could prevent it.

9. In the course of the last four or five years, Miss Lamont has searched for evidence bearing on the story (either by word or picture) in the Archives nationales, in the library, museum, Mairie, and Archives departmentales at Versailles : also in the libraries Nationale, Hôtel de Ville, and in the Musée Carnavalet, and in the Conservatoire de Musique at Paris. She has poked about in French book and print shops, and must have seen a large number of the originals of the published plans, illustrations, and accounts of the place. We

believe that there is not likely to be any striking documentary evidence other than we have dealt with.

10. The historical interest of the story seems to depend on the truth of the tradition that the Queen went to Trianon on October 5th, 1789. We can find no negative evidence of this, but extremely little which is both affirmative and trustworthy. Madame Campan's short statement remains the basis of other people's longer and more detailed narratives. General La Fayette's full account of the day was burned by his wife during the Terror. Count Fersen's memoirs were also partly destroyed. The Abbé Bossuet had Madame de Tourzel's careful history of that day burned; but in the published memoirs she says that she was in residence that day at Versailles, as *Gouvernante des enfants de France*; she does not mention having gone to Trianon, as implied by Marion's story, but it is still possible. Most French historians now adopt Madame Campan's statement, but (in the words of one of them) "with some doubts." It is worth mentioning that many later historians insert the fact (though it is not recorded by Madame

Campan) that "the Queen was accompanied by a single valet." Is this a tradition?

11. We do not believe in anniversaries in the usual sense. We have tested both our days (August 10th and January 2nd), going, as far as possible, under the same circumstances, without any result at the Petit Trianon. Yet it is possible that if we entered into an act of memory, it may well have been first made on the terrible 10th of August, 1792, though the memory itself was occupied (in the central place) with the events of October 5th, 1789. The dress of the messenger was more suitable for October than August. At the same time Vaudreuil left France the previous summer and cannot have sat in the Trianon woods after the taking of the Bastille, July 14th, 1789.

There is an incoherence about both the large and small incidents which seems to require combination within a single mind, and the only mind to which they could all have been present would have been that of the Queen. Our theory of 1901, that we had entered within the working of the Queen's memory when she was still alive, is now enlarged. We think that the two first visits to Trianon (August

10th, 1901, and January 2nd, 1902) were part
of one and the same experience; that quite
mechanically we must have seen it as it appeared to her more than a hundred years ago,
and have heard sounds familiar, and even something of words spoken, to her then.

Having been for two most trying years confined to Paris, and (excepting for a visit to
St. Cloud) through two hot summers, and being
in the midst of the tumultuous horrors of the
great tenth of August, she may, as the day
wore on, and she grew more used to her miser-
able position in the Hall of the Assembly—
where she sat for eighteen hours—have fancied
(in memory) the grounds at Trianon more
spacious than they really were; and have seen
the trees, as one sees trees in recollection, like
a picture without life, depth, or movement.
In rêverie her mind may have wandered from
the familiar sight of the two Bersys at the gate,
to the little vision of two men gathering up
garden rubbish into a cart (which we know
happened on October 5th, 1789, as well as one
day during the last winter she spent at Versailles), and which—without any reason—had
remained in her mind. She may have thought

of the place as it was during that year of the meeting of the States-General when the grounds were, for the first time, thrown completely open to the public, and intruding strangers could be seen there. Or she may have gone back to the earlier years and the pleasant afternoons when the band played on the *pelouse* in front of the house, and to the excitement of acting in the little theatre with her special friends, perhaps letting herself realise the unkindness of the pressure put upon her by Vaudreuil to have the acting of the *Mariage de Figaro* authorised.

How naturally the thought of him would have formed one picture in her mind with the memory of the last scene, when she was hurriedly summoned from Trianon, never to return! For she may very likely have supposed all that she was suffering to have been more exclusively the result of her own former mistakes than could have been just, and have been going over them in her mind.

On our return to Paris on the day of the original visit to Trianon, when undoubtedly her image was uppermost in our thoughts, and the recollection of her terrible end was hardly to be endured, the recurring consolation to Miss Morison was, "She has forgiven it all now, and knows the true meaning of the French Revolution on both its good and bad sides, and also the exact proportion of her own part in it." But the act of memory which had so strangely and mechanically clung to the place, with which we had, perhaps, been associated in the grounds, was incoherent and pictorial. It was oppressive to us because it represented a more limited view of those times than after a hundred years we have learnt to take of them, and was far more limited than any thought the Queen can have about them now.

12. Our answer to the suggestion that we were in a state of suspended consciousness is that our conversation and sense of the quiet continuity of things remained unbroken, and, in spite of oppression, believed ourselves to be particularly wide awake and on the alert. When we were first asked whether the man from the side building was real or not, we laughed at the idea of any un-reality; all was so quietly natural that we are still uncertain whether the tall gardener belonged to another century or not. It has

taken us nine years to work out all the details which bear witness to the strangeness of what we saw and did, and to justify us in our present conviction, that from the moment of our leaving the lane until we emerged into the avenue we were on enchanted ground.

13. The theory of coincidences would have to be considerably strained to cover more than twenty points quickly succeeding one another.

14. In the municipal records kept in the Library at Versailles there is a list of fêtes in the grounds. Miss Lamont has examined it carefully. There had been one for which people had been dressed in Louis XVI. costume in June, 1901, but there is a note to say that it had been confined to the Hameau. There was none in August, 1901. We know that since 1901 there have been fêtes in the grounds with scenes in character, so that other people may have come across them; an examination of the records as to dates would probably reveal such possibilities.

In the same catalogue notices are made of photographs taken of historical groups at fêtes; there had been some in connection with the June fête, and "Otto" was mentioned by name.

On enquiry Otto wrote that he had not taken
"l'ensemble de la fête, c'était des groupes
de jeunes filles, et des dames séparément."
"Dufayel" took pains to look the matter
up, and Miss Lamont and one of his em-
ployées went all through his lists and books
of specimen photographs, and found that he
had not taken any photographs at Trianon
between 1900 and 1906. He recommended
enquiries at Pierre Petit's, as Petit would have
Lafayette's as well as other photographers'
pictures. No photographs of the scenes we
wanted were to be heard of there, and Pierre
Petit wrote afterwards that his only photographs at Trianon had been taken in 1900
for the Exhibition.

It has been suggested to us that our story
can be explained by people posing for a cinematograph in order to register the scene of the
messenger running to the Queen, whilst something further has been said of a girl sweeping
up leaves as forming part of the group. Naturally, from the first, we had thought of some
such explanation, but had rejected it as insuf-
ficient. We did not see the man running; we
only heard him; then he suddenly appeared,

standing close to us, and addressed us personally, earnestly, and with excitement. As a scene it would have been nothing ; we saw no Queen, and no girl sweeping up leaves. He remained by us until we turned away from him. The cinematograph theory does not explain how it was that he came over and stood with his back against rocks of considerable size piled on one another, when rocks have not been there for nearly a hundred years, though we find that they had been placed in that part of the garden in 1788. Nor does it explain how it was that both before and during the man's coming we were both gazing at a kiosk which is not now in existence, though both rocks and kiosk we found out years after to have made part of the original scenery in 1789. Not a word is hinted about the little bridge over the ravine, and the little cascade close by, all being essentials both to our, and, we believe, to the original story. We suspect the explanation to be simply that we had not talked about them at first, not knowing their significance till later, and so they have not got into any widely-spread story. We know from the archives that the streams were not cleared from leaves after October 4th, 1789, and that "Mariamne" is only mentioned as having been paid for work in the grounds in *1783*, as one of several children so occupied.

If masqueraders were posing as guards at the *porte du jardinier*, the cinematograph idea does not explain the reappearance of the old cottage close by, in its former position as placed in Mique's map of 1783. If the part of the Queen was being acted, what of the orchard of trees we saw her looking into, not now in existence; also, what is the account of the barrier at our right hand screening off the present view and exactly answering to the old enclosure of the Jeu de Bague?

The cinematograph does not explain the man who opened the great door of the chapel, easily banging it behind him as he came out; for in 1907 the people living in the place believed that it had not been opened since the days of Louis XVI., and the keeper of the key knew that even the door of the landing had not been opened for fifteen years. How was the wall lowered, which now largely hides the great door from the terrace, and makes it necessary to go down one flight of steps and up another, whereas we saw the man coming along a level, in full view, from the moment of his opening the door until he reached us standing on the terrace outside the window of the *antichambre*?[1]

A cinematograph would not explain the reappearance of the old wood in all its denseness; nor the rapid disappearance of the cart and horse in an open field; nor the music, which, six years later, was found to be a piecing together of eighteenth century operas.

No amount of masqueraders explains to us the ease with which we dismissed from sight and hearing the usual August crowds in the middle of a fine afternoon, and the impossibility of harmonising our recollections of the scenery with anything but the old maps and records. Certainly none of the persons we met were being photographed at the moment, or we must have seen it; and had scenery been erected for the purpose, we must have observed such large artificial arrangements; there would probably have been sightseers; and, presumably, the fact

[1] We heard in 1910 that this was the window out of which Marie Antoinette used to pass when she went into the garden.

of anything so considerable would have been in the catalogue.

Even should it be proved that a cinematograph had been taken that very day, it would not be a possible explanation to us. The groups we saw were small and isolated from one another. There was the deepest silence everywhere, and no sunshine; whilst the light was the worst possible for a picture, for the sky was overcast. And though whilst we stood there an indefinable air of strangeness dropped over everything, including the tall forest trees, it was not of a kind that could be accounted for by fictitious scenery. The people moved and spoke as usual, but their words were extraordinarily difficult to catch.

In September, 1910, the question of such representation was settled by an enquiry of the authorities. No leave to take cinematographs had been granted in August, 1901. The fête had been on June 27th, and the photographs of it had been taken sufficiently near the time to be published in the July number of *Versailles Illustré*. Not one of the pictures in this number is in the least like what we saw either in the matter of subjects, costumes, or places. The inaccuracy is so great, that in an article in the same magazine the scene of the messenger coming to the Queen is transferred from the grotto to the Hameau, though the sole authority for the tradition places it at the grotto.

15. During the last five or six years much research into topographical and archæological details has been made by the newly-formed "Société des amis de Versailles," probably from the same archives examined by Miss Lamont, so that many points of likeness to what we saw may soon reappear. Old music with old-fashioned instruments is now frequently introduced at summer fêtes at Trianon. Even the water arrangements in our part of the garden seem likely to be altered, and the little cascade may yet be seen again. At the beginning of 1910 Miss Lamont saw engineers searching for the first and second *sources,* and in the following autumn she found iron grids placed on the ground near the positions we had allotted for them ; but nothing had been altered up to September, 1910. We are most curious to know whether the restorations will be exactly according to our recollections of the scenery or not.

16. Stories retailing just so much of our own

as we had first talked about are constantly being repeated to us; some with the little additions we can recognise as our own early surmises; generally with the omission of points we did not know to be interesting until later; and often with all the muddles arising from the attempt to shorten a long story, with a few unauthorised additions and explanations thrown in. These stories are told to us as being the property of persons we have never heard of. We have constantly enquired on what authority they rest, and, if there is any at all, we have not infrequently been able to discover the track they have followed from us back to us again.

17. We do not think that deception explains it. If we were deceived in one, two, or three points, could we have been in all? For out of them we have been able to reconstruct the story of Trianon in many tiny details, the truth of which we have had to discover for ourselves.

18. We are constantly asked why we, of all people, should have had such an adventure? We are equally puzzled; and have come to think that it may not be so unusual as it seems. We can imagine that people, even if they suspected anything unusual (which they might

easily not do), may have thought it best not to follow it up. The peculiarity in our case may simply have been that two persons were equally able to consider the circumstances, and did do so : that we found there was available evidence, and that we had the opportunity for obtaining it.

19. Certain unusual conditions were present.

(1) Two people in broad daylight, good health, and normal conditions, were equally able to bear witness to the facts, yet not in the manner of thought transference between each other, for they did not see alike in every point.

(2) Some of the facts were so small that no historical knowledge, however dim, could have suggested them.

(3) They concerned such well known historical personages that much documentary proof as to the reality of the incidents is accessible ; yet, in some particulars, they are of such a nature as to be incapable of reproduction by any tricks of scenic effects ; and some of the evidence found in the archives had, to all appearance, not been disturbed since its collection by the National Assembly until Miss Lamont in 1904 undid the old fastenings that had stuck together

through age and disuse : for instance—much of
the evidence about the gardeners taken from
the wages book.

E. M.

F. L.

September, 1910.

9 781774 642030